The Rapture:

A Pre- or Post-Tribulation Event?

Discover for yourself—through the study of
the Word of God—when the rapture will take
place in the sequence of end-time events

Colleen Wandmacher

ISBN 979-8-88685-227-1 (paperback)
ISBN 979-8-88685-228-8 (digital)

Christian Faith Publishing
832 Park Avenue
Meadville, PA 16335
www.christianfaithpublishing.com

Printed in the United States of America

Dedication

This book is dedicated to the Word of God,
my Lord and Savior, Jesus Christ.
He was with God and was God.
All things were made through him.
He became like one of us to purchase a gift with his life.
His love freely offered me that gift,
the gift of eternal life, purchased with his blood.
He never sinned;
his death paid the penalty for my sins.
He died in my place; now I have life.
He promised me that the sins that once separated me from him
will be remembered no more.
Truly, he is love.
Since the day he saved me, by the power of his Holy Spirit,
he has been giving me understanding of
great and wonderful things from his Word.
He is the Truth, and truths from the Bible,
many passages of which are presented in this book,
are his truths.

Contents

Acknowledgments

In addition to spending countless hours studying end-times on my own, I studied end-times with my very special friend Beth for quite a few years. In search of truth and nothing but the truth, Beth and I rarely studied the teachings of men to find it; rather, we looked to God's Word.

One of the benefits of studying together is that one can confirm or question what the other sees in Scripture. We together saw clear evidence that the rapture would be a post-tribulation event. I don't think I would have written this book had we not both observed the evidence that we did. It confirmed my interpretations. I will be forever grateful that the Lord brought Beth into my life.

Introduction and Instructions

This workbook is for those who are eager to know when—according to the Word of God—the rapture (the catching up of believers to meet the Lord in the air) will take place in the sequence of end-time events. Although God has not made known to us the exact day or hour of the rapture, he has made known to us when it will occur in relation to other events.

According to many, the rapture will be a pre-tribulation event. Since it cannot be denied that the gathering of the elect saints in Matthew 24:31 is a post-tribulation event (see Matthew 24:29–31 below), they must explain away the *gathering* as something other than the rapture. If they were to acknowledge that it was the rapture, they would have to acknowledge that, as Matthew 24 clearly teaches, it will come **after** the time of tribulation, called the Great Tribulation (Revelation 7:14, NASB). If Matthew 24:31 is the rapture, that ends the debate. And there is a lot of evidence that it is.

Jesus said,

> **Immediately after the tribulation** of those days the sun will be darkened, and the moon will not give its light; the stars will fall from heaven, and the powers of the heavens will be shaken. Then the sign of the Son of Man will appear in heaven, and then all the tribes of the earth will mourn, and they will see the Son of Man coming on the

> clouds of heaven with power and great glory. And He will send His angels with a great sound of a trumpet, and they will **gather together His elect** from the four winds, from one end of heaven to the other. (Matthew 24:29–31, NKJV)

But even if it couldn't be proven that Matthew 24:31 is the rapture, there are many other passages that reveal that the rapture will take place at the end of the age—not seven years or so prior to it.

Be a Berean!

It has taken me years to connect the dots and accumulate all the scriptural evidence that is presented in this book. My investigation started around the time I read that we are not supposed to let anyone deceive us in any way and saw that pre-tribulationists explained away what seemed to me to be the clear teaching of 2 Thessalonians 2:1–3.

> Concerning the coming of our Lord Jesus Christ and our being gathered to him, we ask you, brothers, not to become easily unsettled or alarmed by some prophecy, report, or letter supposed to have come from us, saying that the day of the Lord has already come. ***Don't let anyone deceive you in any way***, for that day will not come until the rebellion occurs, and the man of lawlessness is revealed, the man doomed to destruction. (2 Thessalonians 2:1–3)

Paul, an apostle of Jesus, would not have told us to not let anyone deceive us in any way if false teaching about the timing of the rapture was not going to be prevalent. Disturbingly, many (possibly millions) have not taken that admonition seriously. We must remember this: The Holy Spirit enables *all* born-again believers to understand truth. "We have not received the spirit of the world but the Spirit who is from God, that we may understand what God has freely given us" (1 Corinthians 2:12). Jesus wants each one of us to sit at his feet and learn from him, just as Mary did (Luke 10:38–42). He wants us to be Bereans (Acts 17:11). He wants us to study hard. He doesn't want us to put complete trust in any teacher. We need to verify what our teachers teach.

I have heard several people say it isn't important to know whether the rapture will take place before or after the Great Tribulation, but that is to completely ignore these words from 2 Thessalonians 2:3 that were written so that we wouldn't be deceived about the timing: "Don't let anyone deceive you in any way."

I have no interest in trying to talk you into believing what I believe, but God longs for you to believe what he says about the matter. In keeping with that, this workbook was designed to help you be a Berean, one who studies the Scriptures to discover if what he/she has been taught is the truth (Acts 17:10–11). I pray that you will disagree with what is in this book **only** because of something you see in Scripture, not because of what you have been taught by a Bible teacher, a book, a movie, a fine-sounding argument, or an opinion you came up with on your own. I especially pray that fear of persecution won't keep you from seeing the truth.

Because I'm capable of misunderstanding teachings of the Bible and don't know anywhere near all there is to know, it's up to you to check out all my interpretations with the Word of God. This book will help you do that. Determine to believe God's Word alone.

If you study all the passages in this book, I believe you will be totally blown away by the volume of evidence God gave us to show that the rapture will be a post-tribulation event. You will see it in chapter after chapter.

A Pre- or Post-Tribulation Rapture: What Difference Does It Make?

Many believers who have read their Bibles concerning the matter agree with the following:

- Saints **will** be persecuted during the time of great tribulation (Revelation 7:14, Luke 21:12–17, Revelation 13:5–7, Daniel 7:25).

- A rapture event (the catching up of believers to meet the Lord in the air) **will** take place (1 Thessalonians 4:17, 2 Thessalonians 2:1).

What Christians **don't** agree on is the timing of the rapture in the sequence of end-time events. Below are two of the views of the timing of the rapture.

- The pre-tribulation rapture view: the rapture will take place **before** the Great Tribulation, the time of persecution.

- The post-tribulation rapture view: The rapture will take place **after** the Great Tribulation, at the end of the age. Rather than being raptured before then, the saints will enter the time of the reign of the beast and be persecuted, and those who survive will be caught up (raptured) to meet our Lord and those saints who had died beforehand in the air when he returns to the earth to reign as king.

Besides the two views above, there is a pre-wrath view (and a mid-tribulation view, but that view isn't very prevalent). Although those holding the pre-wrath position teach that the rapture will come **before** the end of the age, they **do** believe that God's people alive at the time will enter the time of tribulation and be persecuted and thus need to be spiritually prepared for it.

The Foundation

Before we delve into the Scriptures pertaining to the timing of the rapture, let's look at what the Bible says about the two basic teachings mentioned in the previous section, teachings that many believers agree with:

- A group of saints will be persecuted by the beast (aka the abomination of desolation and the man of lawlessness) during a period of 3.5 years:

  The saints will be handed over to him for a time, times and half a time [3.5 years]. (Daniel 7:25)

  The beast was given a mouth to utter proud words and blasphemies and to exercise his authority for forty-two months [3.5 years]. He opened his mouth to blaspheme God, and to slander his name and his dwelling place and those who live in heaven. He was given power to make war against the saints and to conquer them. And he was given authority over every tribe, people, language and nation. All inhabitants of the earth will worship the beast—all whose names have not been written in the book of life belonging to the Lamb that was slain from the creation of the world. He who has an ear, let him hear. If anyone is to go into captivity, into captivity he will go. If anyone is to be killed with the sword, with the sword he will be killed. This calls for patient endurance and faithfulness on the part of the saints. (Revelation 13:5–10)

- A rapture (the catching up of believers to meet Jesus) will take place:

  But I would not have you to be ignorant, brethren, concerning them which are asleep [which have died], that ye sorrow not, even as others which have no hope. For if we believe that Jesus died and rose again, even so them also which sleep in Jesus will God bring with him. For this we say unto you by the word of the Lord, that we which are alive and remain unto the coming of the Lord shall not prevent [this word means *precede* in modern English] them which are asleep. For the Lord himself shall descend from heaven with a shout, with the voice of the archangel, and with the trump [trumpet call] of God: and the dead in Christ shall rise first: **Then we which are alive and remain shall be caught up together with them in the clouds, to meet the Lord in the air: and so shall we ever be with the Lord.** (1 Thessalonians 4:13–17, KJV)

Those two teachings (there will be a rapture and saints will be persecuted) are the foundation of this study.

Could the Reason Be Fear of Persecution?

The fear of persecution could be one of the reasons Christians are reluctant to believe in a post-tribulation rapture or even study the issue. The apostles of long ago had an entirely different outlook on suffering than some believers of today.

Both Scripture and history teach us that God's children undergo persecution. We are called to follow in the footsteps of Jesus—whom they nailed to a cross. Stephen, the first Christian martyr, was killed for preaching the truth (Acts 7), and millions upon millions have been persecuted since then. In many parts of the world, Christians are being horribly persecuted today.

Have you read *Foxe's Book of Martyrs*? The book tells stories about how God's people—knowing they had eternal life—endured great persecution. The suffering they endured is a taste of what is to come:

> If anyone is to go into captivity, into captivity he
> will go. If anyone is to be killed with the sword,
> with the sword he will be killed. This calls for
> patient endurance and faithfulness on the part of
> the saints. (Revelation 13:10)

Although believers will have to endure the persecution by the beast, they won't have to endure the wrath of God that will be poured out on the Day of the Lord, the last day of the age. (We will explore how God's wrath differs from the hot fury of Satan that will be poured out through the beast during the Great Tribulation.)

Interpretation Chaos

Before we delve into our study, I want to comment on Matthew 24, a chapter that requires careful interpretation. Rather than interpreting it in a vacuum, it's crucially important to use other end-time passages to help understand it, for one wrong interpretation leads to another, then another, then another.

We will dig deeply into parts of Matthew 24, connecting those parts to other passages. I hope you will find it exciting and fulfilling to see how beautifully other pieces of the puzzle lock into place with pieces of Matthew 24.

Be Ready

Here is a question for you: is it important to you to allow God, the lover of your soul, to spiritually prepare you for persecution that may come in your day? If you don't read anything else, be sure to read chapter 11.

This is a good time to offer words of admonishment and encouragement: "Fear not them which kill the body but are not able to kill the soul: but rather fear him which is able to destroy both soul and body in hell" (Matthew 10:28, KJV). The fury of Satan will last only a short time. Those who are persecuted during this time will, after that, be with Jesus forever. God's Word tells us to look forward to the day that it will all be over and gives us the following reason, among many others, to look forward to it:

> You ought to live holy and godly lives as you look forward to the day of God and speed its coming. That day will bring about the destruction of the heavens by fire, and the elements will melt in the heat. **But in keeping with his promise we are looking forward to a new heaven and a new earth, the home of righteousness.** (2 Peter 3:11b–13)

Some Important Things to Keep in Mind

- Except for what is written in Chapter 12, not many attempts were made to argue the points that the pre-tribulation rapture teachers make, as much confusion will be avoided by just concentrating on what God says. A few of the pre-tribulation rapture views are briefly made but only to show why we are studying certain post-tribulation rapture viewpoints.

- A lot of Scriptures quoted are from the King James Version (KJV) of the Bible. Because of the copyright laws and the volume of Scriptures quoted in this workbook, I had to quote many of the Scriptures from a version old enough not to come under those laws. If you are not a KJV lover, I apologize. I am not against the KJV. I just don't prefer to study from it because we don't talk or write like that anymore. Plus, some of the words don't mean the same thing as they do now. For example, the word *prevent* in 1 Thessalonians 4:15 in the KJV means "precede," whereas it means something different in modern English.

- You've heard the statement, "All roads lead to Rome," right? Well, in this book, the chapters pertaining to the timing of the rapture lead to the same conclusion: it will be a post-tribulation event.

- One could study Scriptures pertaining to the end-times and the millennial reign for a hundred years and still have things to learn. The more one studies, the more one can fit together pieces of the puzzle in order to gain understanding of the whole picture. It is important to hang on to the things you see clearly and hold in abeyance your opinion concerning those things you do not yet understand, are not sure about, or don't see evidence of. There are many things about the end-times in Scripture that I do not understand, but presented in this book are things that seem clear to me. Use what is clear to you to be the first properly placed pieces of your puzzle. Even if you don't agree with my understanding, you will find most of the Scriptures needed to form your own opinion in this book.

- Give God's Word full permission to make null and void any false teaching you might be adhering to. Give it time to clear up the confusion you may experience at first while trying to put the pieces of the puzzle into their proper places.

- Some Bible passages are presented and explored more than once in the book, and some things are taught over and over again. Here are my reasons for doing that:

  1. We grasp and/or remember things better by way of hearing them over and over again (at least I do).

  2. We will be looking at how a certain passage links up with other passages because of one aspect of the passage. And then in another chapter, we will be looking at that same passage to see how it links up with other passages because of another aspect of the passage. For example, we will be looking at how a certain passage links up with other passages because of the mention of Jesus coming in the clouds. And then in another chapter, we will be looking at how that same passage links up with other passages because of the mention of a trumpet sound.

  3. I made each chapter that discusses the timing of the rapture as much of a stand-alone chapter as I could; therefore, certain things had to be repeated over and over again.

Must-Read Instructions

- Humble yourself before the Lord, asking him to give you, by the power of his Holy Spirit, understanding of the truth. Be willing to change your mind about a belief that you now hold, no matter who taught it to you, if you see solid evidence in Scripture that contradicts it. **Don't let the word of man, no matter who the man is, blind you to the Word of God.**

- As you study, look for the answers in Scripture alone. Test everything I say with the Word of God. And remember, Bereans are capable of discovering truth. How else could God keep us from being deceived?

  And the brethren immediately sent away Paul and Silas by night unto Berea: who coming thither went into the synagogue of the Jews. These were more noble than those in Thessalonica, in that they received the word with all readiness of mind, and searched the Scriptures daily, [to see] whether those things were so. (Acts 17:10–11, KJV)

- Most of the passages that we will be studying are quoted in the book. If I want you to study a passage that is not in the book, I will mention that you should look it up in your Bible.

- On occasion, you will be asked to fill in a blank with a word from Scripture. Those words are underlined in the quoted Scripture passages so that you can find them more easily. You will also be asked to mark statements true or false or to answer yes or no. Answer according to what you think the Scriptures teach. If you are not sure of an answer, put a question mark there and go back to it later.

- This is important—check things off as you move along so that you will know where you left off.

- Do this study when you are fresh. Your brain will work better.

With a hunger for truth and the help of the Spirit of God, you are about to embark on a journey into the years before and after the end of the age. With your heart and mind fully engaged, read each Bible passage in this book a couple of times over and then answer the questions. Take your time! Enjoy the journey!

Chapter 1

You're So Right, God Did Not Appoint Us to Suffer Wrath!

Paul, in a letter to the Thessalonians, said this to them: "God did not appoint us to suffer wrath [G3709] but to receive salvation through our Lord Jesus Christ" (1 Thessalonians 5:9). But does that mean the rapture will be a pre-tribulation event? Does that mean that believers won't enter the time of tribulation and be persecuted during the Great Tribulation? To answer those questions, we need to look at the ways two different Greek words—G2372 and G3709—have been translated. I contend that G3709 and only G3709 should be translated with the English word *wrath*. Not having done so has blinded us to the fact that G3709 is a specific wrath that will not be poured out until the last day of the age and is the wrath we have not been appointed to suffer.

Read the bullet points below to see what I mean.

- In some of our translations, the same English word *wrath* was used to translate two different Greek words (G2372 and G3709), when there seemingly was no reason for it. For example, in Revelation 14:10 of the King James Version, the Greek word G2372 was translated with the English word *wrath*, and in Revelation 11:18, the Greek word G3709 was also translated with the English word *wrath*. The Greek words G2372 and G3709 are different enough to warrant being translated with different English words. This fact can be seen in verses like this where these words **were** translated with different English words: "And out of his mouth goeth a sharp sword, that with it he should smite the nations: and he shall rule them with a rod of iron: and he treadeth the winepress of the fierceness [G2372] and wrath [G3709] of Almighty God" (Revelation 19:15, KJV).

- In this verse, G2372, in order to differentiate it from G3709, should not have been translated with the word *wrath*: "The devil is come down unto you, having great wrath [G2372], because he knoweth that he hath but a short time" (Revelation 12:12b, KJV).

- Here in the HCSB, the Greek word G3709 **should have been** translated with the English word *wrath*, but was not; instead, it was translated with the word *anger*: "The great city split into three parts, and the cities of the nations fell. Babylon the Great was remembered in God's presence; He gave her the cup filled with the wine of His fierce anger [G3709]" (Revelation 16:19, HCSB).

Because of the inconsistent ways G3709 and G2372 are translated within a version and from version to version, it goes unnoticed that G3709 in 1 Thessalonians 5:9 is a unique wrath that unforgiven humans are storing up for themselves because of their stubborn, unrepentant hearts. It is a wrath that will not be poured out **until** the Day of the God's Wrath when he judges the unrepentant:

> Because of your stubbornness and your unrepentant heart, you are storing up wrath [G3709] against yourself for the **day of God's wrath** [3709], when his **righteous judgment** will be revealed. (Romans 2:5)

As the verse above says, righteous judgment will take place on the Day of God's Wrath. The verse below tells us that this judgment will take place on the Day of Judgment, **when** the heavens and the earth are destroyed.

> By the same word the present heavens and earth are reserved for fire, being kept for the **day of judgment** and destruction of ungodly men. (2 Peter 3:7)

As you can see from marrying Romans 2:5 with 2 Peter 3:7, this stored-up wrath will be released on the Day of Judgment. That day will not come **until** the end of the age when the time has come to destroy the heavens and the earth. Revelation 11:15-18 also reveals that this judgment of sinners will not take place **until** the end of the current age.

Rather than having to suffer the wrath of God on the day that Jesus comes to reign as king of the earth, repentant and saved sinners will receive salvation, just as 1 Thessalonians 5:9 reveals: "God did not appoint us to suffer wrath but to receive salvation through our Lord Jesus Christ." The Bible says we will receive that salvation when Jesus appears a second time (Hebrews 9:28). In other words, rather than receiving wrath that is being stored up for unbelievers, we will receive the last act of our salvation. We will be made like Jesus when we see him (1 John 3:2).

Contrary to popular teaching, it is not the wrath of God that saints will experience during the Great Tribulation; it is Satan's fury [G2372] they will have to endure. "Therefore rejoice, you heavens and you who dwell in them! But woe to the earth and the sea, because the devil has gone down to you! He is filled with **fury**, because he knows that his time is short" (Revelation 12:12). What the saints will experience during Satan's reign through the beast is referred to as *tribulation,* not *wrath* (Matthew 24:9, 21, 29 and Revelation 7:14, NASB).

Looking at the passages below gives believers a correct understanding of what they will be rescued from. Read them and rejoice! For escaping God's wrath (Strong's G3709) means **so much more** than escaping a short period of persecution.

> And the nations were angry, and thy wrath [G3709] is come, and the time of the dead, that they should be judged, and that thou shouldest give reward unto thy servants the prophets, and to the saints, and them that fear thy name, small and great; and shouldest destroy them which destroy the earth. (Revelation 11:18, KJV)

> If any man worship the beast and his image, and receive his mark in his forehead, or in his hand, the same shall drink of the wine of the wrath [Strong's G2372] of God, which is poured out without mixture into the cup of his indignation [the Greek word is Strong's G3709 and thus should have been translated as *wrath*]; and he shall be tormented with fire and brimstone in the presence of the holy angels, and in the presence of the Lamb: and the smoke of their torment ascendeth up for ever and ever: and they have no rest day nor night, who worship the beast and his image, and whosoever receiveth the mark of his name. (Revelation 14:9–11, KJV)

Praise the Lord! Thank the Lord! Our justification has saved us from God's stored-up wrath: "Much more then, being now justified by his blood, we shall be saved from wrath [G3709] through him" (Romans 5:9, KJV).

We shall see in the coming chapters that—just before God's wrath is inflicted upon unrepentant sinners—justified believers who survived the Great Tribulation will be caught up in the air to meet the Lord on his way back to the earth to take his place as king.

Chapter 2
The Last Day Resurrection and Rapture

If you have not read the introduction and instructions (located just before chapter 1), please do so, as there are important things there that you need to know and understand before you read this and other chapters to come.

Don't forget to first read the main passages a couple of times over. And remember that the fill-in-the-blank answers in this and other chapters are underlined in the passages so you can find them easier.

Don't expect complete understanding right away; just pick up details as you journey through the study. A case will be built with those details. Be patient. Don't try to hurry through. Study hard.

Section 1

In this section, we'll study the timing of the resurrection. In section 2, we'll see that the one and only resurrection of the saints and the rapture will take place at almost the same time. And we'll see that they both take place when Jesus comes to reign for a thousand years and not seven or so years prior to that.

Revelation 13:4-7, 15 (KJV)

4 And they worshipped the dragon which gave power unto the beast: and they worshipped the beast, saying, Who *is* like unto the beast? who is able to make war with him?
5 And there was given unto him a mouth speaking great things and blasphemies; and power was given unto him to continue forty and two months [3.5 years].
6 And he opened his mouth in blasphemy against God, to blaspheme his name, and his tabernacle, and them that dwell in heaven.
7 And it was given unto him to make war with the saints, and to overcome them: and power was given him over all kindreds, and tongues, and nations.

15 And he had power to give life unto the image of the beast, that the image of the beast should both speak, and cause that as many as would not worship the image of the beast should be killed.

Revelation 20:4-6 (KJV)

4 And I saw thrones, and they sat upon them, and judgment was given unto them: and I saw the souls of them that were <u>beheaded</u> for the witness of <u>Jesus</u>, and for the word of God, and which had not worshipped the <u>beast</u>, neither his <u>image</u>, neither had received his mark upon their foreheads, or in their hands; and they lived and reigned with Christ a thousand years.

5 But the rest of the dead lived not again until the thousand years were finished. This is the first resurrection.

6 Blessed and holy is he that hath part in the first resurrection: on such the second death hath no power, but they shall be priests of God and of Christ, and shall reign with him a thousand years.

Revelation 7:9-14 (KJV)

9 After this I beheld, and, lo, a great multitude, which no man could number, of all nations, and kindreds, and people, and tongues, stood before the throne, and before the Lamb, clothed with white robes, and palms in their hands;

10 And cried with a loud voice, saying, Salvation to our God which sitteth upon the throne, and unto the Lamb.

11 And all the angels stood round about the throne, and about the elders and the four beasts, and fell before the throne on their faces, and worshipped God,

12 Saying, Amen: Blessing, and glory, and wisdom, and thanksgiving, and honour, and power, and might, be unto our God for ever and ever. Amen.

13 And one of the elders answered, saying unto me, What are these which are arrayed in white robes? and whence came they?

14 And I said unto him, Sir, thou knowest. And he said to me, These are they which came out of great tribulation, and have washed their robes, and made them white in the blood of the Lamb.

Matthew 24:9, 15, 21 (KJV)

9 Then shall they deliver you up to be afflicted, and shall kill you: and ye shall be hated of all nations for my name's sake.

15 When ye therefore shall see the abomination of desolation, spoken of by Daniel the prophet, stand in the holy place, (whoso readeth, let him understand).

21 For then shall be great tribulation, such as was not since the beginning of the world to this time, no, nor ever shall be.

John 6:39-40 (NASB)

39 This is the will of Him who sent Me, that of all that He has given Me I lose nothing, but raise [resurrect] it up on the last day.
40 For this is the will of My Father, that _everyone_ who beholds the Son and believes in Him will have eternal life, and I Myself will raise him up on the _last_ day.

Before we discover when the rapture will take place, we will look into when the resurrection will take place, as they will both occur at nearly the same time.

- ☐ We see in Revelation 13:15 that those who do not worship the image of the beast will be killed. ☐ True ☐ False

- ☐ According to Revelation 13:5–7, the beast's reign, the time during which he makes war with the saints, will last forty-two months (3.5 years). ☐ True ☐ False

❏ According to Revelation 20:4, souls were _______________ _______________ for the "witness of _______________." They were beheaded because they did not worship the _______________ or his _______________ during his reign.

❏ Does Revelation 20:6 speak of the resurrection? _______________ And does that resurrection take place just before the thousand-year reign of Jesus? _______________

❏ Now look at Matthew 24:21. Will there be a period of great tribulation? _______________

❏ According to Matthew 24:9, 15, and 21, will the saints be killed and hated for Jesus's name's sake during the reign of the abomination of desolation (aka the beast), the period of great tribulation? _______________

❏ According to Revelation 7:9 and 14, saints from all over the globe will come out of the Great Tribulation. ❏ True ❏ False

❏ From the passages you just studied, would you say the beast's reign of forty-two months (3.5 years) is the period of great tribulation we read about in the Matthew 24 passage? _______________

❏ If the saints are killed for refusing to worship the beast during the 3.5 years of tribulation, it follows then that they won't be resurrected until after the Great Tribulation. ❏ True ❏ False

❏ I just learned that the day of resurrection of those saints killed for not worshiping the beast will take place **after** the 3.5-year Great Tribulation, just **before** the thousand-year reign of Christ, which means the resurrection will take place at the end of the age. ❏ True ❏ False

Now that we have studied that, we will look for even more evidence that the resurrection will take place at the end of the age—not years prior to the end. Sit tight. After that, we will see crystal clear evidence that the rapture will take place on the same day as the resurrection. If they take place on the same day, the rapture, like the resurrection, will take place at the end of the age—after the Great Tribulation. In other words, it will be a post-tribulation event.

- ☐ According to John 6:39, those who were given to Jesus by his Father will be raised up on the last day. ☐ True ☐ False

- ☐ According to John 6:40, ________________________ who beholds the Son and believes in Him will be raised on the last day.

- ☐ So then, according to John 6:40, **all** believers will be raised up on the _____________ day.

- ☐ If **all** believers are raised on the same day, there will be **only one** resurrection day, and it will take place "on the last day" (John 6:40). ☐ True ☐ False

Section 2

Okay, now let's find out what will happen on the **same day** as the resurrection of the saints.

---

1 Thessalonians 4:13-17 (KJV)

13 But I would not have you to be ignorant, brethren, concerning them which are asleep [which have died], that ye sorrow not, even as others which have no hope.
14 For if we believe that Jesus died and rose again, even so them also which sleep in Jesus will God bring with him.
15 For this we say unto you by the word of the Lord, that we which are alive and remain unto

the coming of the Lord shall not prevent [precede] them which are asleep.

16 For the Lord himself shall descend from heaven with a shout, with the voice of the archangel, and with the trump [trumpet call] of God: and the dead in Christ shall rise first:

17 Then we which are alive and remain shall be caught up together with them in the clouds, to meet the Lord in the air: and so shall we ever be with the Lord.

(1 Corinthians 15:50-53 KJV)

50 Now this I say, brethren, that flesh and blood cannot inherit the kingdom of God; neither doth corruption inherit incorruption.

51 Behold, I shew you a mystery; We shall not all sleep, but we shall all be changed,

52 In a moment, in the twinkling of an eye, at the last trump: for the trumpet shall sound, and the dead shall be raised incorruptible, and we shall be changed.

53 For this corruptible must put on incorruption, and this mortal must put on immortality.

❏ According to 1 Thessalonians 4:14, who will God bring with Jesus when He comes?

❏ According to 1 Thessalonians 4:17, what insanely exciting thing will happen to those who are still alive and remain? (Note: Christians call this event the rapture.)

❑ According to 1 Thessalonians 4:16, who will rise (be resurrected) first?

❑ According to 1 Thessalonians 4:16–17, will those who are still alive be caught up (raptured) to meet the Lord in the air **immediately after** the resurrection of those who had by this time fallen asleep (died)? ___________ Will those **two** things (the resurrection of those who had died and the rapture of those who are alive and left) take place after the trumpet call of God is heard (verse 16)? ___________

❑ According to 1 Corinthians 15:52, what two things will happen after the trumpet sounds?

❑ Did you learn from the 1 Corinthians 15 passage that **after the trumpet sounds,** the dead will be raised and immediately afterward believers will be changed? ___________ And did you learn from the 1 Thessalonians 4 passage that **after the trumpet sounds** the dead will be raised and immediately afterward those alive and left will be raptured? ___________ Thus, they must be speaking of the same event. ❑ True ❑ False

❑ Putting the details of the 1 Corinthians 15 passage and the 1 Thessalonians 4 passage together, we learn that those alive and left will be raptured and changed **at nearly the same time** that those who had died are resurrected. ❑ True ❑ False

❑ The changing of those still alive will take place because "flesh and blood cannot inherit the kingdom of God" (1 Corinthians 15:50). These saints must be changed when they are raptured so that they will then have immortal bodies, like the resurrected ones, and thus be prepared to inherit the kingdom of God. ❑ True ❑ False

❏ I learned from section 1 that **all** believers will be raised (resurrected) **on the last day**, the day that marks the end of the age and the beginning of the thousand-year reign of Jesus Christ. I learned from this section that the rapture and the changing of those raptured will take place on the **same day** as the resurrection. That means the rapture, likewise, will take place on the last day. ❏ True ❏ False

Read again the passages quoted in this chapter. Read slowly and think deeply, asking the Lord to reveal to you what he is saying. Afterward, check the following summary statements you agree with:

❏ Those who are alive and left when Jesus returns will be raptured on the same day as the resurrection. Thus, what is true about the timing of the resurrection is true about the timing of the rapture:

- The resurrection will take place <u>after</u> the Great Tribulation.

- The resurrection will take place <u>on</u> the last day.

- The resurrection will take place <u>when</u> Jesus returns to reign for a thousand years.

❏ Therefore, the rapture will be an end-of-the-age, beginning-of-the-new-age, post-tribulation event that will take place when Jesus returns to reign for a thousand years.

Record here anything that you disagree with or are not sure about:

____

____

____

____

Chapter 3
The Last Trumpet

Matthew 24:29–31, from one of our *trumpet* passages, states,

> 29 **Immediately after the tribulation of those days** the sun will be darkened, and the moon will not give its light; the stars will fall from heaven, and the powers of the heavens will be shaken. 30 Then the sign of the Son of Man will appear in heaven and then all the tribes of the earth will mourn, and they will see the Son of Man coming on the clouds of heaven with power and great glory. 31 And He will send His angels with a great sound of a trumpet, and **they will gather together His elect** from the four winds, from one end of heaven to the other.

Because pre-tribulationists claim that the rapture will take place before the tribulation mentioned in Matthew 24:29, they must explain away Matthew 24:31 as being something **other than** the rapture. That is because the gathering mentioned in that verse will take place after—not before—the "tribulation of those days," which is called, according to Matthew 24:21, the *Great Tribulation* (see the main Matthew 24 passage).

What they teach makes it necessary for post-tribulationists like me to prove that Matthew 24:31 is indeed speaking of the rapture. That will be done in this chapter by tying certain *trumpet* passages together. (Scriptural evidence will be provided in other chapters as well.) Let's see if you agree that Matthew 24:31 must be describing the rapture.

Please allow me to explain once again that you will see some of the same details over and over again. That is because the timing of the rapture is proven in different ways using some of the same Scriptures.

So that you can spot them easier in each of the *trumpet* passages in this chapter, the words *trumpet* and *trump* are in bold typeface.

Section 1

---

1 Thessalonians 4:15-17 (KJV)

15 For this we say unto you by the word of the Lord, that we which are alive and remain unto the coming of the Lord shall not prevent [precede] them which are asleep.
16 For the Lord himself shall descend from heaven with a shout, with the voice of the archangel, and with the **trump [trumpet]** of God: and the dead in Christ shall rise first:
17 Then we which are alive and remain shall be caught up together with them in the clouds, to meet the Lord in the air: and so shall we ever be with the Lord.

Matthew 24:3, 9-10, 14-21, 29-31 (NKJV)

3 Now as He [Jesus] sat on the Mount of Olives, the <u>disciples</u> came to Him privately, saying, "Tell us when will these things be? And what will be the sign of Your coming, and of the end of the age?"

9 Jesus said, "Then they will deliver you up to <u>tribulation</u> and kill you, and you will be <u>hated</u> by all nations for <u>My</u> name's sake.

10 "And then many will be offended, will betray one another, and will hate one another.

14 "And this gospel of the kingdom will be preached in all the world as a witness to all the nations and then the end will come.

15 "Therefore when you see the 'abomination of desolation,' spoken of by Daniel the prophet, standing in the holy place (whoever reads, let him understand),

16 "then let those who are in Judea flee to the mountains.

17 "Let him who is on the housetop not go down to take anything out of his house.

18 "And let him who is in the field not go back to get his clothes.

19 "But woe to those who are pregnant and to those who are nursing babies in those days!

20 "And pray that your flight may not be in winter or on the Sabbath.

21 "For then [when we see the abomination of desolation] there will be great tribulation, such as has not been since the beginning of the world until this time, no, nor ever shall be.

29 "Immediately after the tribulation of those days the sun will be darkened, and the moon will not give its light; the stars will fall from heaven, and the powers of the heavens will be shaken.

30 "Then the sign of the Son of Man will appear in heaven and then all the tribes of the earth will mourn, and they will see the Son of Man coming

> on the clouds of heaven with power and great
> glory.
> **31** "And He will send His angels with a great
> sound of a **trumpet**, and they will gather together
> His elect from the four winds, from one end of
> heaven to the other."

First, let's examine verses from 1 Thessalonians 4 and Matthew 24 to see how these two passages tie together because of the sound of a trumpet.

- ☐ Read 1 Thessalonians 4:15–17, and then answer these questions: Do you agree that a trump (trumpet) will be heard when the Lord comes? _____________ Do you agree that those who are alive and remain will be caught up (raptured) to meet those who have died and the Lord Jesus in the air **at the sound of that trumpet?** _________

- ☐ Read Matthew 24:30–31, and then answer these questions: Do you agree that a trumpet will be heard when Jesus comes? _________ Do you agree the elect (the saints) will be gathered from one end of heaven to the other **at the sound of that trumpet?** _________

- ☐ Is there a place in the Bible, besides Matthew 24:31, that refers to this event as a gathering? (Hint: See 2 Thessalonians 2:1 *in your Bible*.) _________ With the evidence presented so far, would you say that Matthew 24:30–31, because of the way it ties to 1 Thessalonians 4:15–17, is likely speaking of the rapture, calling it a gathering, as does 2 Thessalonians 2:1? _________

Second, now let's look at one more way the passages link together. Answer the following regarding 1 Thessalonians 4:15–17 and Matthew 24:30–31:

- ☐ Both passages say Jesus will come **in the clouds.** ☐ True ☐ False

☐ Now we have tied the passages together in another way. With this additional evidence, would you say that Matthew 24:30–31 is more than likely speaking of the rapture? __________

Third, let's now look at verses in the Matthew 24 passage that will help us determine who it is that will be gathered when a trumpet sound is heard and the timing of the gathering in the sequence of end-time events.

☐ According to Matthew 24:3, Jesus was talking to his ________________ when he told them about the persecution to come, the abomination of desolation, and his return.

☐ According to Matthew 24:9, Jesus said, "They will deliver you [the disciples] up to _____________________________ and kill you, and you will be ________________ by all nations for _______ name's sake."

☐ Pre-tribulationists (at least some of them) say the Book of Matthew was written to the Jewish people and not to the church. They say that it is so because the church didn't exist yet. Therefore, according to them, Jesus was speaking not to the church but to Jewish people (who they say will be saved after a supposed pre-tribulation rapture) when he spoke of the coming persecution (Matthew 24:9). Let's test that claim: Look up Matthew 16:18 and 18:17 *in your Bible*. Was the church mentioned in those verses? __________

☐ Pre-tribulationists say the church will be raptured seven years or so prior to the end of the age, an age that ends with the return of Jesus (see Matthew 24:3 and 30). In numerous ways, we will test that in coming chapters, but let's test it here with a passage from the Book of Matthew. In Matthew 28:19–20 (look it up *in your Bible*), was Jesus telling the church to make disciples of all the nations to the **very end of the age**? __________ Does that mean the church will be here to the end of the age? __________

❏ Read Matthew 24:29–31 with some of the words left out: "Immediately after the tribulation of those days… He will send His angels…and they will gather together His elect." Now answer this question: Does that passage, without a doubt, reveal that the elect are gathered (raptured) after the days of tribulation? ___________

❏ Therefore, according to Matthew 24, Jesus's disciples will be killed and hated (verse 9) during the Great Tribulation (verses 9, 21, and 29), and those who survive will be gathered (raptured) immediately after the time of tribulation (verses 29–31), making it a post-tribulation event. ❏ True ❏ False

Section 2

So far, we have tied together two trumpet passages. But let's not stop there. Let's find more proof of a post-tribulation rapture by looking at two more passages that contain the word *trumpet* and comparing them to our 1 Thessalonians 4 trumpet/rapture passage.

---

1 Corinthians 15:50-53 (KJV)

50 Now this I say, brethren, that flesh and blood cannot inherit the kingdom of God; neither doth corruption inherit incorruption.

51 Behold, I shew you a mystery; We shall not all sleep, but we shall all be changed,

52 In a moment, in the twinkling of an eye, at the last **trump**: for the **trumpet** shall sound, and the dead shall be raised incorruptible, and we shall be changed.

53 For this corruptible must put on incorruption, and this mortal must put on immortality.

---

1 Thessalonians 4:15-17 (KJV)

15 For this we say unto you by the word of the Lord, that we which are alive and remain unto the coming of the Lord shall not prevent [precede] them which are asleep.
16 For the Lord himself shall descend from heaven with a shout, with the voice of the archangel, and with the **trump [trumpet]** of God: and the dead in Christ shall rise first:
17 Then we which are alive and remain shall be caught up together with them in the clouds, to meet the Lord in the air: and so shall we ever be with the Lord.

Revelation 11:15-18 (KJV)

15 And the <u>seventh</u> angel sounded [his **trumpet**]; and there were great voices in heaven, saying, The kingdoms of this world are become the kingdoms of our Lord, and of his Christ; and he shall reign for ever and ever.
16 And the four and twenty elders, which sat before God on their seats, fell upon their faces, and worshipped God,
17 Saying, We give thee thanks, O Lord God Almighty, which art, and wast, and art to come; because thou hast taken to thee thy great power, and hast reigned.
18 And the nations were angry, and thy wrath is come, and the time of the dead, that they should be judged, and that thou shouldest give reward unto thy servants the prophets, and to the saints, and them that fear thy name, small and great; and shouldest destroy them which destroy the earth.

Let's compare the 1 Corinthians 15, 1 Thessalonians 4, and Revelation 11 passages.

- ☐ Does 1 Corinthians 15:52 say—**at the sound of a trumpet**—the dead will be raised? __________

- ☐ Does 1 Thessalonians 4:16 say—**at the sound of a trumpet**—the dead will be raised? __________

- ☐ We learned in chapter 2 that there will be only one resurrection day, which will take place on the last day. Since there is only one resurrection day, 1 Thessalonians 4:16 and 1 Corinthians 15:52 must both be speaking of the same resurrection, the one and only resurrection that will take place on the last day when the trumpet sounds. ☐ True ☐ False

- ☐ According to 1 Corinthians 15:52, what will happen to those yet alive when the dead are raised at the sound of a trumpet?

- ☐ According to 1 Thessalonians 4:16–17, what will happen to those yet alive when the dead are raised at the sound of a trumpet?

- ☐ Do you agree that both 1 Corinthians 15:52 and 1 Thessalonians 4:16-17 relate that the resurrection will occur at almost exactly the same time as the changing/rapture? __________

With the above said, let's dig deeper.

- ☐ According to 1 Corinthians 15:52–53, will those who are raised from the dead and those who are changed become immortal? __________ According to 1 Corinthians 15:50–53, can only the immortal inherit the kingdom of God? __________

❏ According to Revelation 11:15, it is when the ________________________ angel sounds his trumpet (the last trumpet sound in a series of seven trumpet sounds) that the kingdoms of the world become the kingdoms of our Lord.

❏ According to 1 Corinthians 15:52–53, it is when the ________________ trumpet sounds that the dead and the others (the changed ones) become immortal.

❏ Therefore, does it seem likely to you that the last trump of 1 Corinthians 15:52 is the seventh trumpet sound of Revelation 11:15 and that, put together, the passages tell us that those who are changed from mortal to immortal will inherit the kingdom of God when the kingdoms of the world become the kingdom of our Lord? __________ And does Revelation 11:15 tell us that the seventh angel will sound his trumpet at the beginning of the reign of Jesus? __________

Note: While Revelation 11:15–18 doesn't mention the rapture, it is interesting to note that it is at the sounding of the seventh trumpet and the return of Christ to take over the world that the saints are rewarded (see verse 18).

❏ Let's put the passages in this section together: The 1 Corinthians 15 and 1 Thessalonians 4 passages tell us that at the sound of a trumpet, the dead will be raised and, immediately afterward, those still alive will be raptured and changed. The 1 Corinthians 15 passage says this will happen at the sound of the *last* trumpet. It also says only those who have immortal bodies will inherit the kingdom of God. Revelation 11:15 says that at the sound of the seventh trumpet (the last in a series of seven trumpets) "the kingdoms of the world will become the kingdoms of our Lord, and of his Christ." From these passages, we can say that the rapture will not take place until the sounding of the last (seventh) trumpet when the kingdoms of world become the kingdom of God. ❏ True ❏ False

Section 3

In section 1, we tied together some things in two trumpet passages: the 1 Thessalonians 4 and the Matthew 24 passage. In section 2, we tied together the 1 Corinthians 15, 1 Thessalonians 4, and Revelation 11 passages. We did this because linking passages allows Scripture to interpret Scripture. It enables puzzle pieces to be locked into their proper places. It eliminates the need to explain away the meaning of certain Scriptures.

❒   Do you agree that we have pretty good evidence to tie all these passages together? ❏ I agree ❏ I disagree

Having studied these select passages, please now take the time to review the following chart to see all that takes place at the sound of a trumpet:

PASSAGE REFERENCE	THE LIVING SAINTS...	THIS WILL TAKE PLACE...	THIS WILL HAPPEN...
1 Thessalonians 4:16–17	...will be raptured just after those who have died are resurrected.	...when Jesus comes in the clouds.	...at the <u>trumpet</u> call of God.
1 Corinthians 15:50–52	...will be changed (become immortal).	...because flesh and blood cannot inherit the kingdom of God.	...when the last <u>trumpet</u> sounds.
Revelation 11:15–18	...will be rewarded.	...when the kingdoms of the world become the kingdom of our Lord and of his Christ.	...when the seventh <u>trumpet</u> sounds.

Matthew 24:9–31	…will be gathered (raptured) by angels.	…when Jesus comes in the clouds, *after* the time that the elect are persecuted, a time known as the Great Tribulation.	…at the sound of a <u>trumpet</u>.

Note: Read 2 Thessalonians 1:3–5 *in your Bible* to find out why the saints who inherit the kingdom will be worthy of the kingdom.

Mark the following statement true or false:

❑ Looking at what each of the four passages says about what will take place when the sound of a trumpet is heard and linking the passages together reveals that current-age saints will enter and be persecuted during the time of the Great Tribulation. After that, when it is time for the kingdoms of the world to become the kingdoms of our Lord and of his Christ, the seventh trumpet will sound. Our Lord will return in the clouds, the dead will be raised, and those yet alive will be changed and raptured to meet them and our Lord in the air. ❑ True ❑ False

Record here anything that you disagree with or are not sure about:

____

____

____

____

____

____

Chapter 4
The Clouds

In the preceding chapter, we focused primarily on how certain passages tie together because of the mention of a trumpet sound. Now we are going to link certain passages together because of the mention of Jesus coming in the clouds.

If the cloud passages should be linked together, Jesus will come in the clouds only once. Thus, this is how events will play out:

> Scenario no. 1: Saints will see the abomination of desolation. Those who die during the Great Tribulation, a time that will begin when he stands in the holy place claiming to be God, will be blessed (Revelation 14:13). Those who survive will have the extreme joy of being caught up to meet Jesus when he comes in the clouds to set up his kingdom. At that time, the Lord will pour out his wrath on the sinners who chose to worship the beast (the abomination of desolation).

If the cloud passages shouldn't be linked together, Jesus will come twice in the clouds. Thus, this is how events will play out:

> Scenario no. 2: Jesus will come a second time and a third time. He will come in the clouds and the saints of the church will be caught up to meet

him. They will not be here to see the abomination of desolation stand in the holy place. Nor will they be here during the Great Tribulation, the time of the persecution of the saints. Jesus will come a third time. This time too he will come in the clouds, at which time he will set up his kingdom and destroy those who chose to worship the beast (the abomination of desolation).

After you study this chapter, you will be given an opportunity to choose whether you believe scenario no. 1 or scenario no. 2 to be the true scenario.

Let me remind you again that, as you go through this workbook, you will find that certain things are repeated over and over again. The four reasons for that are the following: (1) We are looking at some of the same passages from different angles. (2) We learn and grow in our understanding by hearing things over and over again. (3) Each timing chapter was written, to a degree, to be a stand-alone chapter, so it was necessary to write those chapters with some of the same explanations and/or linking evidence as in other chapters. (4) The timing chapters were written to prove the same thing—the rapture will be an end-of-the-age, post-tribulation event.

The word *cloud* and the word *clouds* in the passages below are in bold typeface so that you can easily spot them.

Section 1

Matthew 24:9, 15-16, 21, 29-31 (NKJV)

9 [Jesus said,] "Then they will deliver you up to *tribulation* and kill you, and you will be hated by all nations for My name's sake.

15 "Therefore when you see the '*abomination of desolation*,' spoken of by Daniel the prophet, standing in the holy place" (whoever reads, let him understand),
16 "then let those who are in Judea flee to the mountains.

21 "For then [when we see the abomination of desolation] there will be *great tribulation*, such as has not been since the beginning of the world until this time, no, nor ever shall be.

29 "Immediately after the *tribulation* of those days the sun will be darkened, and the moon will not give its light; the stars will fall from heaven, and the powers of the heavens will be shaken.
30 "Then the sign of the Son of Man will appear in heaven and then all the tribes of the earth will mourn, and they will see the Son of Man coming on the **clouds** of heaven with power and great glory.
31 "And He will send His angels with a great sound of a trumpet, and they will *gather together* His elect from the four winds, from one end of heaven to the other."

---

1 Thessalonians 4:16-17 (KJV)

16 For the Lord himself shall descend from heaven with a shout, with the voice of the archangel, and with the trump of God: and the dead in Christ shall rise first:
17 Then we which are alive and remain shall be caught up together with them in the **clouds**, to meet the Lord in the air: and so shall we ever be with the Lord.

Acts 1:1-11 (KJV)

1 The former treatise have I made, O Theophilus, of all that Jesus began both to do and teach,

2 Until the day in which he was taken up, after that he through the Holy Ghost had given commandments unto the apostles whom he had chosen:

3 To whom also he shewed himself alive after his passion by many infallible proofs, being seen of them forty days, and speaking of the things pertaining to the kingdom of God:

4 And, being assembled together with them, commanded them that they should not depart from Jerusalem, but wait for the promise of the Father, which, saith he, ye have heard of me.

5 For John truly baptized with water; but ye shall be baptized with the Holy Ghost not many days hence.

6 When they therefore were come together, they asked of him, saying, Lord, wilt thou at this time restore again the kingdom to Israel?

7 And he said unto them, It is not for you to know the times or the seasons, which the Father hath put in his own power.

8 But ye shall receive power, after that the Holy Ghost is come upon you: and ye shall be witnesses unto me both in Jerusalem, and in all Judaea, and in Samaria, and unto the uttermost part of the earth.

9 And when he had spoken these things, while they beheld, he was taken up; and a **cloud** received him out of their sight.

10 And while they looked stedfastly toward heaven as he went up, behold, two men stood by them in white apparel;

> **11** Which also said, Ye men of Galilee, why stand ye gazing up into heaven? this same Jesus, which is taken up from you into heaven, shall so come in like manner as ye have seen him go into heaven.

First, let's notice how three of the main passages above link together.

- ❏ Look below. Notice that verses from the three passages mention Jesus's coming.

  - Matthew 24:30 says, "They will see the Son of Man **coming**."

  - First Thessalonians 4:16 (KJV) says, "For the Lord himself **shall descend from heaven**."

  - Acts 1:11 says, "Which also said, Ye men of Galilee, why stand ye gazing up into heaven? this same Jesus, **which is taken up from you into heaven, shall so come in like manner** as ye have seen him go into heaven."

- ❏ Look below. Notice that verses from the three passages mention either one or multiple clouds.

  - Matthew 24:30 says, "They will see the Son of Man coming on the **clouds**."

  - First Thessalonians 4:17 (KJV) says, "Then we which are alive and remain shall be caught up together with them in the **clouds**, to meet the Lord in the air: and so shall we ever be with the Lord."

  - Acts 1:9–11 reveals that Jesus will return in the same way that he left, that is, in a **cloud**.

❏ Look below. Notice that verses from two of the main passages say believers will be gathered together.

- First Thessalonians 1:17 says believers will be **caught up together**.

- Matthew 24:31 says the elect will be **gathered together**.

Important note: Matthew 24:31 is not the only verse that describes the event as a gathering of the saints at the coming of Jesus. Second Thessalonians 2:1 does too: "Concerning the coming of our Lord Jesus Christ and our being gathered to him…" (2 Thessalonians 2:1).

Linking passages together allows Scripture to interpret Scripture. It enables puzzle pieces to be locked into their proper places. It eliminates the need to explain away the clear meaning of Scripture.

❏ Do you agree that we have pretty good evidence to tie all three passages together? ❏ I agree ❏ I disagree

❏ We will study the Acts 1 passage more in a minute, but for now, respond to this: If 1 Thessalonians 4:16–17 describes the rapture, then Matthew 24:31 likely does also. ❏ True ❏ False

❏ In the Matthew 24 passage, circle the emphasized word *tribulation* in verse 9 and 29. Circle the emphasized words *abomination of desolation* in verse 15. Circle the emphasized words *great tribulation* in verse 21. Circle the words *gather together* in verse 31. Analyze the passage. Then answer this question: Does the chronology of the Matthew 24 passage make it clear that the gathering of the elect that Matthew 24:31 mentions will take place after the persecution of the saints during the reign of the abomination of desolation, a time referred to as the Great Tribulation? __________ Therefore, the gathering will be a post-tribulation event. ❏ True ❏ False

Now let's take a closer look at the Acts 1 passage for the purpose of determining if Jesus will come in the clouds one more time or two more times.

- ❐ According to Acts 1:6–11, the disciples wanted to know when Jesus would restore the kingdom to Israel. Jesus said it wasn't for them to know the times or the seasons. However, two angels told the disciples that Jesus would come back in the same way they saw him go into heaven—that is, in a cloud. ❑ True ❑ False

- ❐ Read Acts 1:6–11 again, and then mark this statement true or false: Because of what Jesus and the angels said to the disciples, they understood that believers would see Jesus coming in a cloud when the time came for him to restore the kingdom to Israel—not years before that. ❑ True ❑ False

- ❐ Let's find out what Acts 1 doesn't say: Did Jesus tell his followers they would see him come in the clouds to rapture them before he came in the clouds to restore the kingdom to Israel?

- ❐ According to Acts 3:21 (quoted below), Jesus will not leave heaven **until** it is time to restore everything. ❑ True ❑ False

  > He must remain in heaven until the time comes
  > for God to restore everything, as he promised
  > long ago through his holy prophets. (Acts 3:21)

- ❐ From Acts 1:6–11 and Acts 3:21, we learn that Jesus will remain in heaven **until** such time as he comes in a cloud to restore the kingdom to Israel. ❑ True ❑ False

- ❐ Considering what we just learned about how Jesus won't leave heaven and return in a cloud until it is time to restore the kingdom to Israel and remembering that we tied Matthew 24:30–31 with 1 Thessalonians 4:16–17 (two other cloud passages), it has to be that Matthew 24:30–31 depicts the rapture that will take place at the one and only second coming of Jesus in the clouds. (Jesus came the first time two thousand years ago.) ❑ True ❑ False

Note: For more on why the return of Jesus prophesied in Acts 1:6–11 and 3:21 will not take place until the end of the age, see section 2 of chapter 10.

Second, let's put together what we have learned so far so we don't get lost in the details.

- ❑ The 1 Thessalonians 4 passage says Jesus will come in the clouds. The passage details the rapture. ❑ True ❑ False

- ❑ The Acts 1 passage says Jesus will come in a cloud when it comes time to restore the kingdom to Israel. ❑ True ❑ False

- ❑ The Acts 3:21 says he will not leave heaven before that. ❑ True ❑ False

- ❑ Matthew 24:31 speaks of the angels collecting the elect as a gathering; 2 Thessalonians 2:1, a rapture passage, does as well. ❑ True ❑ False

- ❑ The Matthew 24 passage says Jesus will come in the clouds and angels will gather (rapture) the elect **after** the reign of the abomination of desolation, the time of great tribulation. ❑ True ❑ False

Section 2

We are going to look at one more cloud passage, Revelation 14:6–20, along with one supporting non-cloud passage.

Revelation 14:6-20 (KJV)

6 And I saw another angel fly in the midst of heaven, having the everlasting gospel to preach unto them that dwell on the earth, and to every nation, and kindred, and tongue, and people,

7 Saying with a loud voice, Fear God, and give glory to him; for the hour of his judgment is come: and worship him that made heaven, and earth, and the sea, and the fountains of waters.

8 And there followed another angel, saying, Babylon is fallen, is fallen, that great city, because she made all nations drink of the wine of the wrath of her fornication.

9 And the third angel followed them, saying with a loud voice, If any man worship the beast and his image, and receive his mark in his forehead, or in his hand,

10 The same shall drink of the wine of the wrath [this word is G2372, and should have been translated with a word other than the word *wrath* in order to distinguish it from G3709] of God, which is poured out without mixture into the cup of his indignation [this word is G3709 and should have been translated the word *wrath*, as were other G3709 Greek words]; and he shall be tormented with fire and brimstone in the presence of the holy angels, and in the presence of the Lamb:

11 And the smoke of their torment ascendeth up for ever and ever: and they have no rest day nor night, who worship the beast and his image, and whosoever receiveth the mark of his name.

12 Here is the patience of the saints: here are they that keep the commandments of God, and the faith of Jesus.

13 And I heard a voice from heaven saying unto me, Write, <u>Blessed</u> are the dead which die in the Lord from henceforth: Yea, saith the Spirit, that they may rest from their labours; and their works do follow them.
14 And I looked, and behold a white *cloud*, and upon the *cloud* one sat like unto the Son of man, having on his head a golden crown, and in his hand a sharp sickle.
15 And another angel came out of the temple, crying with a loud voice to him that sat on the *cloud*, Thrust in thy sickle, and reap: for the time is come for thee to reap; for the harvest of the earth is ripe.
16 And he that sat on the *cloud* thrust in his sickle on the earth; and the earth was reaped.
17 And another angel came out of the temple which is in heaven, he also having a sharp sickle.
18 And another angel came out from the altar, which had power over fire; and cried with a loud cry to him that had the sharp sickle, saying, Thrust in thy sharp sickle, and gather the clusters of the vine of the earth; for her grapes are fully ripe.
19 And the angel thrust in his sickle into the earth, and gathered the vine of the earth, and cast it into the great winepress of the wrath of God.
20 And the winepress was trodden without the city, and blood came out of the winepress, even unto the horse bridles, by the space of a thousand and six hundred furlongs.

In the passage above, we read about the reaping of the believing, patient saints (verses 12–16, highlighted in gray). We also read about the gathering and the destruction of unbelievers (verses 18–20). In the text, the prophecy of the reaping of the believers comes just before the prophecy of the gathering and destruction of the unbelievers. Therefore, if the destruction of the unbelievers comes at the end of the age, then so does the reaping of the believers. Seems reasonable, right? Let's explore.

Message for Unbelievers

If you are not saved, it would be good to think about this: You are completely helpless to save yourself; however, God, whom all love comes from, did *all* that was necessary to save you.

Eternal life is a free gift, a gift that was paid for by Jesus with his life. He died in your place on that "old rugged cross." The cup of God's wrath and eternal torment will be poured out only on those who reject the salvation that Jesus, God in the flesh, freely offers us. Long ago, Jesus said this to a Samaritan woman standing near a well: "If you knew the gift of God and who it is that asks you for a drink, **you would have asked him** and he would have given you living water" (John 4:10). Read chapter 13 to learn more about how you can receive this most amazing gift and freedom from not just the punishment of sin but the power of sin.

Before we investigate the Revelation 14 passage, it will be good for you to understand (if you don't already) God's character and why some day, he will punish those who had refused to love the truth and so be saved (2 Thessalonians 2:10). God sent his Son, Jesus, who came voluntarily, to die for all our sins so that they could be washed away and no longer separate us from him. By that act, he demonstrated his love for us and showed us what love is. Although the creator of all things, the one who is love, the perfectly wise one, the all-knowing one deserves our worship, he won't force us to worship him. He, having done all that was necessary that we might live with him for all eternity and become holy by his power, humbly allows us to reject him and live apart from him forever. He allows those who wish to remain under the control of Satan to do so.

Having reflected a bit on the character of God, let's reflect on the character of Satan. He is a liar, a thief, a destroyer, and a murderer (John 8:44 and 10:10). He has been deceiving the world since deceiving Eve in the garden of Eden. One of the most effective lies he tells, if not **the** most effective, is that man is good enough to earn his way to heaven. Toward the end of the age, he is going to give the beast his authority and will demand that everyone on the face of the earth worship him. By worshiping the beast, they will be worshiping Satan. Since Satan has done nothing worthy of worship, he must demand it. He will not allow anyone who does not worship him to buy or sell anything at all.

Although God invites all to live forever with him and did all that was necessary to make that possible (Revelation 22:17), he can't allow those who choose to worship the beast and delight in being wicked to be a part of his forever family.

Having reflected now both on the character of God and Jesus and the character of Satan and the beast, let's look into Revelation 14.

First, let's look at the passage to see what will happen to those who worship the beast.

- ❒ According to Revelation 14:6, will the eternal gospel be preached to the entire world? _________

- ❒ According to Revelation 14:9–11, is mankind warned not to worship the beast? _________ According to Revelation 14:7, is mankind told to worship God who made heaven and earth? _________

- ❒ Does it make all the sense in the universe to reject a created, wicked being and worship the one who is love and the creator of all that has been created? _________

❏ According to Revelation 14:10, those who worship the beast will be tormented when it becomes time to drink the wine of God's wrath. ❏ True ❏ False

❏ According to Revelation 14:17–19, one angel told another angel that it was time to gather the clusters of grapes from the earth's vine. Where, according to verse 19, will the grapes be thrown?

Second, let's study what will happen to those who worship God, according to Revelation 14:12–16, which was couched between the two sections pertaining to the fate of those who worship the beast.

❏ According to Revelation 14:12–16,

"Here is the patience of the ___________________: here are they that _____________ the commandments of God, and the faith of ________________. And I heard a voice from heaven saying unto me, Write, ___________________ are the dead which in the Lord from henceforth: Yea, saith the Spirit, that they may rest from their labours; and their works do follow them. And I looked, and behold a white ________________, and upon the ________________ one sat like unto the Son of man, having on his head a golden crown, and in his hand a sharp sickle. And another angel came out of the temple, crying with a loud voice to him that sat on the ________________, Thrust in thy sickle, and reap: for the time is come for thee to reap; for the harvest of the earth is ripe. And he that sat on the ________________ thrust in his sickle on the earth; and the earth was reaped."

Third, now let's think about the **timing** of the reaping of believers when Jesus comes in a cloud and the gathering of the unbelievers to throw them into the winepress of the wrath of God:

☐ After studying Revelation 14:14-20, would you say that the believers are reaped **just before** the unbelievers are gathered to be thrown into the great winepress of the wrath of God? _______________ Therefore, because unbelievers are destroyed at the end of the age, the reaping of believers must occur at the end of the age, not seven years before then. ☐ True ☐ False

Fourth, let's look at more evidence that (a) the saints will be reaped (gathered) and (b) sinners punished at the coming of Jesus in a cloud. This will support the fact that the reaping of the saints will occur at nearly the same time that those who had worshiped the beast are thrown into the winepress of the wrath of God.

We are going to explore this non-cloud supporting passage (below) in depth in coming chapters, but let's briefly review it now. Read it, and then mark true or false the statement that follows the passage:

> **They will be punished** with everlasting destruction and shut out from the presence of the Lord and from the majesty of his power **on the day he comes** to be glorified in his holy people and to be marveled at among all those who have believed... **Concerning the coming of our Lord Jesus Christ and our being gathered to him**, we ask you, brothers, not to become easily unsettled or alarmed by some prophecy, report or letter supposed to have come from us, saying that the day of the Lord has already come. (2 Thessalonians 1:9–10, 2:1–2)

❏ The 2 Thessalonians passage above says saints will be gathered (raptured) and sinners destroyed. **Both** will take place **when** our Lord Jesus comes. ❏ True ❏ False

---

Now mark which of the following scenarios you believe Scripture teaches:

❏ Scenario no. 1: The saints will see the abomination of desolation. Those who die during the Great Tribulation, a time that will begin when he stands in the holy place claiming to be God, will be blessed (Revelation 14:13). Those who survive will have the extreme joy of being caught up to meet Jesus when he comes in the clouds to set up his kingdom. At that time, the Lord will pour out his wrath on the sinners who chose to worship the beast (the abomination of desolation).

❏ Scenario no. 2: Jesus will come a second time and a third time. He will come in the clouds and the saints of the church will be caught up to meet him. They will not be here to see the abomination of desolation stand in the holy place. Nor will they be here during the Great Tribulation, the time of the persecution of the saints. Jesus will come a third time. This time, too, he will come in the clouds, at which time he will set up his kingdom and destroy those who choose to worship the beast (the abomination of desolation).

Record here anything that you disagree with or are not sure about:

____

____

____

____

Chapter 5

The Great Day of God's Wrath

The passages in this chapter will reveal that the following days all refer to the same day, a day I will call the **Great Day of God's Wrath**.

- the Day of God

- the Great Day of His Wrath

- the Great Day of God Almighty

- the Great and Dreadful Day of the Lord

- the (Day of the) Wrath of Almighty God

The chapter will also reveal that the Day of the Lord is the same day as the Great Day of God's Wrath. Each of the "Day of…" passages details events of the end of the age, the time of God's wrath. By looking at the end-of-the-age events that will take place on this day, we will see that the rapture, because it will occur on the Day of the Lord, will occur at the very end of the age—not years prior to the end.

As was said earlier in the book, we are looking at the timing of the rapture from different angles, and this chapter looks at it from yet another angle.

Revelation 6:12-17 (KJV)

12 And I beheld when he had opened the sixth seal, and, lo, there was a great earthquake; and the sun became black as sackcloth of hair, and the moon became as blood;

13 And the stars of heaven [the sky] fell unto the earth, even as a fig tree casteth her untimely figs, when she is shaken of a mighty wind.

14 And the heaven [sky] departed as a scroll when it is rolled together; and every mountain and island were moved out of their places.

15 And the kings of the earth, and the great men, and the rich men, and the chief captains, and the mighty men, and every bondman, and every free man, hid themselves in the dens and in the rocks of the mountains;

16 And said to the mountains and rocks, Fall on us, and *hide us from the face of him that sitteth on the throne, and from the wrath [G3709] of the Lamb*:

17 For **the great day of his wrath** [G3709] is come; and who shall be able to stand?

Revelation 16:13-21 (KJV)

13 And I saw three unclean spirits like frogs come out of the mouth of the dragon, and out of the mouth of the beast, and out of the mouth of the false prophet.

14 For they are the spirits of devils, working miracles, which go forth unto the kings of the earth and of the whole world, to gather them to the battle of that **great day of God Almighty.**

15 Behold, *I [Jesus] come as a thief.* Blessed is he that watcheth, and keepeth his garments, lest he walk naked, and they see his shame.

16 And he gathered them together into a place called in the Hebrew tongue Armageddon.

17 And the seventh angel poured out his vial into the air; and there came a great voice out of the temple of heaven, from the throne, saying, It is done.

18 And there were voices, and thunders, and lightnings; and there was a great earthquake, such as was not since men were upon the earth, so mighty an earthquake, and so great.

19 And the great city was divided into three parts, and the cities of the nations fell: and great Babylon came in remembrance before God, to give unto her the cup of the wine of the fierceness of his wrath [G3709].

20 And every island fled away, and the mountains were not found.

21 And there fell upon men a great hail out of heaven, every stone about the weight of a talent: and men blasphemed God because of the plague of the hail; for the plague thereof was exceeding great.

Revelation 19:11-21

11 *And I saw heaven opened, and behold a white horse; and he that sat upon him was called Faithful and True,* and in righteousness he doth judge and make war.

12 His eyes were as a flame of fire, and on his head were many crowns; and he had a name written, that no man knew, but he himself.

13 And he was clothed with a vesture dipped in blood: and his name is called The Word of God.

14 And the armies which were in heaven followed him upon white horses, clothed in fine linen, white and clean.

15 And out of his mouth goeth a sharp sword, that with it he should smite the nations: and he shall rule them with a rod of iron: and he treadeth the winepress of the fierceness and **wrath [3709] of Almighty God.**

16 And he hath on his vesture and on his thigh a name written, King of Kings, And Lord Of Lords.

17 And I saw an angel standing in the sun; and he cried with a loud voice, saying to all the fowls that fly in the midst of heaven, Come and gather yourselves together unto the supper of the great God;

18 That ye may eat the flesh of kings, and the flesh of captains, and the flesh of mighty men, and the flesh of horses, and of them that sit on them, and the flesh of all men, both free and bond, both small and great.

19 And I saw the beast, and the kings of the earth, and their armies, gathered together to make war against him that sat on the horse, and against his army.

20 And the beast was taken, and with him the false prophet that wrought miracles before him, with which he deceived them that had received the mark of the beast, and them that worshipped his image. These both were cast alive into a lake of fire burning with brimstone.

21 And the remnant were slain with the sword of him that sat upon the horse, which sword proceeded out of his mouth: and all the fowls were filled with their flesh.

---

2 Peter 3:10-12 (KJV)

10 But the **day of the Lord** will come as a thief in the night; in the which the heavens shall pass away with a great noise, and the elements shall melt with fervent heat, the earth also and the works that are therein shall be burned up.
11 Seeing then that all these things shall be dissolved, what manner of persons ought ye to be in all holy conversation and godliness,
12 Looking for and hasting unto the coming of the **day of God**, wherein the heavens being on fire shall be dissolved, and the elements shall melt with fervent heat?

Isaiah 13:9-13 (KJV)

9 Behold, the **day of the Lord** cometh, cruel both with wrath and fierce anger [3709, according to *The Apostolic Bible Polyglot*], to lay the land desolate: and he shall destroy the sinners thereof out of it.
10 For the stars of heaven and the constellations thereof shall not give their light: the sun shall be darkened in his going forth, and the moon shall not cause her light to shine.
11 And I will punish the world for their evil, and the wicked for their iniquity; and I will cause the arrogancy of the proud to cease, and will lay low the haughtiness of the terrible.
12 I will make a man more precious than fine gold; even a man than the golden wedge of Ophir.

13 Therefore I will shake the heavens, and the earth shall remove out of her place, *in the wrath of the Lord of hosts*, and in the day of his fierce anger [3709, according to *The Apostolic Bible Polyglot*].

Joel 2:31

31 The sun will be turned to darkness and the moon to blood before the coming of the **great and dreadful day of the Lord.**

---

2 Thessalonians 1:8-10; 2:1-2

Chapter 1
8 He will punish those who do not know God and do not obey the gospel of our Lord Jesus.
9 They will be punished with everlasting destruction and shut out from the presence of the Lord and from the majesty of his power
10 on the day he comes to be glorified in his holy people and to be marveled at among all those who have believed. This includes you, because you believed our testimony to you.

Chapter 2
1 Concerning *the coming of our Lord Jesus Christ* and our being gathered to him, we ask you, brothers,
2 not to become easily unsettled or alarmed by some prophecy, report or letter supposed to have come from us, saying that the **day of the Lord** has already come.

Chapter 4

16 For *the Lord himself shall descend from heaven* with a shout, with the voice of the archangel, and with the trump [trumpet call] of God: and the dead in Christ shall rise first:

17 Then we which are alive and remain shall be caught up together with them in the clouds, to meet the Lord in the air: and so shall we ever be with the Lord.

18 Wherefore comfort one another with these words.

Chapter 5

1 But of the times and the seasons, brethren, ye have no need that I write unto you.

2 For yourselves know perfectly that the **day of the Lord** so cometh as a thief in the night.

3 For when they shall say, Peace and safety; then sudden destruction cometh upon them, as travail upon a woman with child; and they shall not escape.

First, let's analyze and link together the three Revelation passages to see if they all refer to the same day, and then we'll see what that tells us. The word *wrath* (G3709) in each of these passages is—in the original language of the New Testament—the same word. It is G3709 in *The Strong's Strongest Exhaustive Concordance of the Bible*. (See chapter 1 for more details regarding this wrath that believers have not been appointed to suffer.)

Grab a yellow, pink, green, blue, and orange highlighter or crayon or pencils. (If you don't have highlighters, pencils, or crayons in those colors, mark them in other colors or some other way.)

- ☐ Link no. 1

  - ☐ In Revelation 6:14, **highlight in yellow** "every mountain and island were moved out of their places."

  - ☐ In Revelation 16:20, **highlight in yellow** "every island fled away, and the mountains were not found."

- ☐ Link no. 2

  - ☐ In Revelation 6:17, **highlight in pink** "the great day of his wrath [G3709]."

  - ☐ In Revelation 16:14, **highlight in pink** "that great day of God Almighty."

  - ☐ In Revelation 19:15, **highlight in pink** "wrath [G3709] of Almighty God."

- ☐ Link no. 3

  - ☐ In Revelation 6:16, **highlight in green** "the Lamb," who is Jesus.

  - ☐ In Revelation 16:15, **highlight in green** "I [Jesus]."

  - ☐ In Revelation 19:13, **highlight in green** "The Word of God," which is another name for Jesus.

- ☐ Link no. 4

  - ☐ In Revelation 6:15, **highlight in blue** "kings of the earth, and the great men, and the rich men, and the chief captains, and the mighty men, and every bondman, and every free man."

❑ In Revelation 16:14, **highlight in blue** "kings of the earth and of the whole world."

❑ In Revelation 19:18, **highlight in blue** "the flesh of kings, and the flesh of captains, and the flesh of mighty men, and the flesh of horses, and of them that sit on them, and the flesh of all men, both free and bond, both small and great."

❑ Link no. 5

    ❑ In Revelation 16:14, **highlight in orange** "to gather them to the battle."

    ❑ In Revelation 19:19, **highlight in orange** "gathered together to make war."

❑ Link no. 6

    ❑ In Revelation 6:17, **underline** "wrath [3709]."

    ❑ In Revelation 16:19, **underline** "wrath [3709]."

    ❑ In Revelation 19:15, **underline** "wrath [3709]."

❑ Taking your time, look at what you highlighted and look at what you underlined. After seeing the commonalities in the three Revelation passages that you just examined, do you concur that they must refer to the same day? __________

❑ If you concurred that the Revelation passages refer to the same day, is it okay if we refer to that day, called by names that are a bit different, as the Great Day of God's Wrath in the rest of this chapter? __________

❑ Besides the fact that men are gathered together, the mountains and islands are removed, and Jesus returns, what are other things that will happen, according to Revelation 6:12–14, Revelation

16:19, and Revelation 19:20–21 on this day of wrath? (These events are highlighted in gray so that you can find them easier.)

❏ It's obvious that the Revelation passages speak of the **last day of the age** because the stars fall to the earth, the sky departs, the mountains and islands are removed, the world's cities collapse, etc. ❏ True ❏ False

Second, now we'll see if linking the passages together will reveal that the Day of the Lord is the same day as the Great Day of God's Wrath.

❏ Look at what each bullet point **below** says about what will happen to the sun and the moon. Does it make sense to link those passages together? ___________ Because of the way they link together, we have evidence that the Day of the Lord is the Great Day of God's Wrath. ❏ True ❏ False

- Isaiah 13:10, from a <u>Day of the Lord</u> passage, tells us that the sun will be darkened and the moon will not shine.

- Joel 2:31, a <u>Great and Dreadful Day of the Lord</u> verse, tells us that the sun will turn dark and the moon will turn to blood.

- Revelation 6:12, from a <u>Great Day of His Wrath</u> passage, tells us that the sun will turn black and the moon will turn to blood.

❏ After looking at what each bullet point **below** says about what will happen to sinners, including the sinful kings of the earth and their armies, on a particular day, answer this question: Do we have even more evidence that the Day of the Lord is the same day as the Great Day of God's Wrath? ___________

- Revelation 6:15–17, from a <u>Great Day of His Wrath</u> passage, tells us that the kings of the earth and those with them will see him who sits on the throne and the Lamb and realize they will not be able to stand.

- Revelation 19:19–21, from a <u>Wrath of Almighty God</u> passage, tells us that the kings of the earth and their armies will be killed.

- Isaiah 13:9 and 11, from a <u>Day of the Lord</u> passage, tells us that sinners will be destroyed; the **world** will be punished.

- The Second Letter to Thessalonians 1:8–9, from a <u>Day of the Lord</u> passage, tells us that those who do not know God will be punished with everlasting destruction.

- The First Letter to Thessalonians 5:3, from a <u>Day of the Lord</u> passage, tells us that destruction will come upon sinners.

❏ Look at what each bullet point below says about what will happen on and to the earth. Should the passages that reveal those things be linked together? __________ Does linking these passages together help reveal that the Day of the Lord is the same day as the Great Day of God's Wrath? __________

- Revelation 6:14, from a <u>Great Day of His Wrath</u> passage, tells us that every mountain and island will be moved out of their place.

- Revelation 16:19–20, from a <u>Great Day of God Almighty</u> passage, tells us that the cities of the nations will fall, every island will flee away, and the mountains will not be found.

- Second Peter 3:10, from a <u>Day of the Lord</u> passage, tells us that the earth will be burned up.

- • Isaiah 13:9, from a <u>Day of the Lord</u> passage, tells us that the land will be made desolate.

❐ Check out each one of the passages referenced below to see if they speak of the coming of Jesus, either explicitly or implicitly? (I have italicized the mention of his coming in each of the passages so you can find it easier.) Does the fact of his coming link the passages together? ___________ Now look below to see what kind of passage each of them is. Thus, without a doubt, the Day of the Lord is the Great Day of God's Wrath. ❏ True ❏ False

- • Revelation 6:12–17 is a Great Day of His Wrath passage.

- • Revelation 16:13–21 is a Great Day of God Almighty passage.

- • Revelation 19:11–21 is a Wrath of Almighty God passage.

- • The Second Letter to Thessalonians 1:8–2:2 is a Day of the Lord passage.

- • The First Letter to Thessalonians 4:16–5:3 is a Day of the Lord passage.

❐ Have we seen that the Day of the Lord is the same day as the Great Day of God's Wrath? ___________

❐ Observe these two main passages, pretending the man-made chapter breaks are not there: the entire 2 Thessalonians passage (verses from both chapters) and the entire 1 Thessalonians passage (verses from both chapters). Would you say that the rapture/gathering will take place on the Day of the Lord? ___________

❐ We linked in several ways the Day of the Lord passages with the Day of God's Wrath passages. Because the rapture will take place on the Day of the Lord and the end-of-the-age events (stars falling, sinners being destroyed, the earth being burned up, etc.) will occur on the same day, the rapture, likewise, will be an end-of-the-age event. ❑ True ❑ False

---

You don't have to answer any more questions in this chapter. Just review, if you wish, all the end-of-the-age events that will take place on the Day of the Lord (aka the Great Day of God's Wrath) and then notice that the rapture also will occur on this same day.

❑ The Revelation 6 passage relates the following will take place on the <u>Great Day of His Wrath</u>:

- The sun will turn black (verse 12).

- The moon will become as blood (verse 12).

- The stars will fall from the *sky* (translated as heaven) to the earth (verse 13).

- The *sky* (translated as heaven) will recede like a scroll (verse 14).

- Every mountain and island will be moved out of their places (verse 14).

- The kings and the others will see him who sits on the throne and the Lamb, and they will call to the mountains and the rocks saying, "Fall on us, and hide us from the face of him that sitteth on the throne, and from the wrath of the Lamb!" (verses 15–16).

❑ The Revelation 16 passage relates the following will take place on the <u>Great Day of God Almighty</u>:

- The kings of the whole world will gather for battle (verse 14).

- Jesus will come (verse 15).

- The cities of the nations will fall (verse 19).

- Every island will flee and the mountains will not be found (verse 20).

❒ The Revelation 19 passage relates that the following will take place on the (Day of the) <u>Wrath of God Almighty</u>:

- The Word of God (Jesus) will come down from heaven on a white horse (verses 11 and 13).

- The beast, the kings of the earth, and their armies will be gathered together to make war against Jesus and his army (verse 19).

- The beast and the false prophet will be thrown into a lake of fire (verse 20).

- The rest will be killed with the sword of Jesus's mouth (verse 21).

❒ The 2 Peter 3 passage relates that the following will take place on the <u>Day of the Lord</u> (also called the Day of God):

- The heavens will pass away (verse 10).

- The earth will be burned up by fire (verse 10).

❒ The Isaiah 13 passage relates that the following will take place on the <u>Day of the Lord</u>:

- The stars of heaven and their constellations will not show their light (verse 10).

- The rising sun will be darkened, and the moon will not give its light (verse 10).

- Sinners will be destroyed (verse 9 and 11).

❏ The 2 Thessalonians 1 and 2 passage relates the following will take place on the <u>Day of the Lord</u>:

- Jesus will come (verse 2:1).

- The saints will be *gathered/raptured* (verse 2:1).

- Those who do not know God will be destroyed (1:8 and 9).

❏ The 1 Thessalonians 4 passage relates the following will take place on the <u>Day of the Lord</u>:

- Jesus will come (verse 4:16).

- The saints will be *raptured* (verse 4:17).

- Sinners will be destroyed (verse 5:3).

Record here anything that you disagree with or are not sure about:

____

____

____

____

By the way, do you find that your learning soars when you link Bible passages together in this way? Does the task of putting details together from passages that link make sense considering that Jesus tells us we need every word that comes from God (Matthew 4:4)? It's as if he was saying we need every piece of the puzzle to see the whole picture.

Chapter 6

The Day of the Lord

We studied various "Day of…" passages in chapter 5. In this chapter, we will study only "Day of the Lord" passages.

In sections 1 and 2, we'll unearth more evidence that (a) the second coming of Jesus in the clouds, (b) the rapture, (c) the destruction of the beast, and (d) the destruction of the world and the sinners therein will occur on the **same day**, **the last day of the age**, a day referred to as the Day of the Lord in the passages we are going to study. You may be surprised by all there is to learn from just one passage, the 2 Thessalonians passage.

In section 3, we will learn that the Day of the Lord and the Great Tribulation are two distinct periods of time. You'll see why we need to learn this when we get to that section.

Section 1

We briefly examined part of the following passage in a previous chapter, but we will examine it in much more detail in this chapter.

Chapter 1

3 We ought always to thank God for you, brothers, and rightly so, because your faith is growing more and more, and the love every one of you has for each other is increasing.

4 Therefore, among God's churches we boast about your perseverance and faith in all the persecutions and trials you are enduring.

5 All this is evidence that God's judgment is right, and as a result you will be counted worthy of the kingdom of God, for which you are suffering.

6 God is just: He will pay back trouble to those who trouble you

7 and give relief to you who are troubled, and to us as well. This will happen when the Lord Jesus is revealed from heaven in blazing fire with his powerful angels.

8 He will punish those who do not know God and do not obey the gospel of our Lord Jesus.

9 They will be punished with everlasting destruction and shut out from the presence of the Lord and from the glory of his might

10 on the day he comes to be glorified in his holy people and to be marveled at among all those who have believed. This includes you, because you believed our testimony to you.

11 With this in mind, we constantly pray for you, that our God may count you worthy of his calling, and that by his power he may fulfill every good purpose of yours and every act prompted by your faith.

12 We pray this so that the name of our Lord Jesus may be glorified in you, and you in him, according to the grace of our God and the Lord Jesus Christ.

Chapter 2

1 Concerning the coming of our Lord Jesus Christ and our being gathered to him, we ask you, brothers,

2 not to become easily unsettled or alarmed by some prophecy, report or letter supposed to have come from us, saying that the **day of the Lord** has already come.

3 Don't let anyone deceive you in any way, for that day [the Day of the Lord] will not come until the rebellion occurs and the man of lawlessness is revealed, the man doomed to destruction.

4 He will oppose and will exalt himself over everything that is called God or is worshiped, so that he sets himself up in God's temple, proclaiming himself to be God.

5 Don't you remember that when I was with you I used to tell you these things?

6 And now you know what is holding him back, so that he may be revealed at the proper time.

7 For the secret power of lawlessness is already at work; but the one who now holds it back will continue to do so till he is taken out of the way.

8 And then the lawless one will be revealed, whom the Lord Jesus will overthrow with the breath of his mouth and destroy by the splendor of his coming.

9 The coming of the lawless one will be in accordance with the work of Satan displayed in all kinds of counterfeit miracles, signs and wonders,

10 and in every sort of evil that deceives those who are perishing. They perish because they refused to love the truth and so be saved.

11 For this reason God sends them a powerful delusion so that they will believe the lie
12 and so that all will be <u>condemned</u> who have not believed the truth but have <u>delighted</u> in <u>wickedness</u>.

First, we are going to study the 2 Thessalonians 1 and 2 passage thoroughly to see what will take place on the Day of the Lord. We will learn other things as well from the passage.

- ❐ According to 2 Thessalonians 1:3, what was happening to the faith and love of these true Christians?

- ❐ According to 2 Thessalonians 1:4, we learn that God allows Christians to be persecuted. ❐ True ❐ False

- ❐ According to 2 Thessalonians 1:4, what did Paul boast about?

- ❐ *Open your Bible* and read Luke 9:22–26. What is Jesus saying?

A Word of Encouragement

"Rejoice that you participate in the sufferings of Christ, so that you may be overjoyed when his glory is revealed" (1 Peter 4:13).

According to 2 Thessalonians 1:6–7:

- ❐ Who will God pay back trouble to?

❏   When will he pay them back?

❏   Who will God give relief to?

❏   When will he give them relief?

❏   Therefore, he will pay back trouble to those who trouble believers and give relief to believers who were troubled **on the same day**, for verses 6–7 say that both will happen "when the Lord Jesus is revealed from heaven." ❏ True ❏ False

❏   According to 2 Thessalonians 1:9–10, will unbelievers be punished with everlasting punishment on the day Jesus comes? _____________ According to 2 Thessalonians 2:1, will believers be gathered to the Lord **on that same day**, on the day Jesus comes? _____________

❏   Read 2 Thessalonians 1:9–2:2 (pretending that the man-made chapter break does not exist), focusing on verses 1:9–10 and 2:1–2. Now fill in the blanks in this sentence: the day that unbelievers are punished with everlasting destruction and believers are gathered (raptured) to Jesus when he comes is called, according to verse 2:2, "the _____________ _____________ _____________ _____________."

❏   According to 2 Thessalonians 2:8, who will be destroyed by the splendor of Jesus's coming? _____________ _____________ _____________. If the lawless one is destroyed by the splendor of Jesus's **coming** and Jesus **comes** on the Day of the Lord, then it must be that the lawless one will be destroyed on the Day of the Lord. ❏ True ❏ False

❑ If unbelievers are punished and the lawless one destroyed on the Day of the Lord, then would you say that this day must take place at the end of the age, not seven years or so prior to it? __________ If the rapture, likewise, takes place on the Day of the Lord, the rapture will take place at the end of the age. ❑ True ❑ False

❑ Read 2 Thessalonians 2:1–9, and then answer these questions: We are not to let __________________ deceive us in __________ __________. God's Word says the Day of the Lord, which is the day that Jesus gathers us, will not occur until **after** the rebellion and the revealing of the lawless one when he "sets himself up in God's temple, proclaiming himself to be God." ❑ True ❑ False

❑ Therefore, those Christians still alive will be here to see the rebellion and the revealing of the lawless one. Until the rebellion takes place and the lawless one is revealed, we will know that the coming of Jesus and the gathering of believers to him has not yet occurred. ❑ True ❑ False

❑ Read 2 Thessalonians 2:8-9 and then answer these questions: According to verse 9, "Will the coming of the lawless one will be in accordance with the work of Satan displayed in all kinds of counterfeit miracles, signs and wonders." __________ Therefore, along with the revealing of the lawless one (when he stands in the temple claiming to be God), there will be signs, wonders, and miracles that occur before the rapture. ❑ True ❑ False

Second, let's compare some things from the Book of Second Thessalonians with Matthew 24:3 and 15 to confirm that believers will still be here to see the man of lawlessness, who is also called the abomination of desolation. Here we go. Let's allow Scripture to confirm Scripture.

❑ Now *open your Bible* and read Matthew 24:3 and 15. Was Jesus telling his **disciples** that they would see the abomination of desolation (aka the man of lawlessness) standing in the holy place (i.e., the temple)? _____________ Is it disciples that make up the church? _____________

☐ See 2 Thessalonians 1:1 *in your Bible*. Was Paul's letter addressed to the church? _____________ It goes without saying, but is it the church who will see the lawless one? _____________

☐ Therefore, **both** 2 Thessalonians and Matthew 24 reveal that it is Jesus's disciples (aka the church) who will see the man of lawlessness in the temple. ☐ True ☐ False

☐ Read Matthew 24:15 and 29–31 *in your Bible*. Now answer this question: Will the disciples see the abomination of desolation (verse 15) **before** the coming of Jesus and the gathering (verses 29–31)? _____________ Does that agree with what 2 Thessalonians 2:1–3 says? _____________ Does that help prove that the Day of the Lord (in other words, the day of the coming of the Lord and the rapture) will not take place until **after** the man of lawlessness is revealed? _____________

☐ Some who believe in a pre-tribulation rapture are forced to deny that the church will still be here to see the lawless one and be persecuted during his reign, a time called the Great Tribulation. If the things we learned in this section are true, there will be no pre-tribulation coming of Jesus, just a post-tribulation coming on the Day of the Lord. ☐ True ☐ False

☐ Do you think, according to 2 Thessalonians 2:3, the deception about the timing of the gathering (rapture) was expected to be pervasive? _____________

☐ According to 2 Thessalonians 2:1–3, would you say that Paul, speaking by the Holy Spirit, is trying to keep believers from being deceived about the timing of the Lord's coming and the gathering (the rapture) of believers to Jesus? _____________

☐ Biblically speaking, a tradition is a man-made teaching. Jesus says this to those who hand down man-made teachings: "Thus you nullify the word of God by your tradition that you have handed down" (Mark 7:13). Because man-made teachings make void the Word of God, it is important to study the Scriptures, like the Bereans of Acts 17:10–11, to identify any handed-down, man-made traditions we may have been taught. ☐ True ☐ False

☐ Now read Matthew 16:21–23 *in your Bible*. The passage is about Peter and Jesus. But let's think about what pre-tribulationist teachers tell us. Is it possible for a good leader who doesn't like the idea of someone having to be persecuted to err with regard to the timing of the rapture? __________ According to verse 23, what does Jesus say to Peter?

According to Matthew 16:24–27 (read it *in your Bible*):

☐ What must a person who wants to be Jesus's disciple do?

☐ Who will lose their life?

☐ The one who loses their life is the one who forfeits their soul. ☐ True ☐ False

☐ Will those who are willing to follow Jesus be rewarded for what they do? ________ When will they be rewarded?

❏ Read 2 Timothy 4:3–5 *in your Bible*, and then answer this question: According to verse 3, will a time come when men will not put up with sound doctrine (teaching)? _________ According to that same passage, do some tend to gather around them teachers who will say what their ears want to hear? _________ According to verse 4, will they turn their ears away from the truth? _________ According to verse 5, are believers called to endure hardship? _________ Do many of our teachers tell us we will be raptured before the hardships of the Great Tribulation occur? _________ Do our ears want to hear that? _________

❏ Are our great Bible teachers infallible? _________ According to Galatians 2:11 (look it up *in your Bible*), was Peter (aka Cephas), an apostle, ever found to be in error? _________

❏ Does Jesus, the one who loves you perfectly, want you to allow **anyone** in **any way** to deceive you about the matter of the timing of the coming of Jesus and the rapture? _________

As long as we are studying the 2 Thessalonians passage, let's learn other things from it.

❏ According to 2 Thessalonians 2:10, why will people perish?

❏ Answer this: Rather than make the choice to refuse to love the truth, can a person make the choice to love the truth and be saved? _________

❏ According to 2 Thessalonians 2:9–10, "Those who are perishing" will be deceived by "counterfeit miracles, signs and wonders, and in every sort of evil." ❏ True ❏ False

❏ According to 2 Thessalonians 2:12, "All will be _________ _________________ who have not believed the truth but have ________________ in ___________________."

Message for Unbelievers

Second Peter 3:9 says that God is "not willing that any should perish." If you do not delight in wickedness and would like God to forgive and change you, please read Chapter 13 to find out what you must believe to be saved. It isn't a matter of what you must **do**; it's a matter of what you must **believe**. After you believe and already have eternal life, God will give you His power to **do** good works. "It is by grace you have been saved, through faith—and this not from yourselves, it is the gift of God—not by works, so that no one can boast. For we are God's workmanship, created in Christ Jesus to do good works, which God prepared in advance for us to do" (Ephesians 2:8–10).

☐ Would living with Jesus for all eternity be wonderful for God's people if those who delighted in wickedness were allowed to live with them? ___________

Section 2

The 1 Thessalonians passage below is a "Day of the Lord" passage, but because we have looked at this passage a couple of times already, we will just take a quick peek to remind ourselves of what this, the clearest rapture passage in the Bible, says about what will happen on the Day of the Lord.

```
1 Thessalonians 4:13-5:4, 5:9-10 (KJV)
```

Chapter 4
13 But I would not have you to be ignorant, brethren, concerning them which are asleep, that ye sorrow not, even as others which have no hope.

14 For if we believe that Jesus died and rose again, even so them also which sleep in Jesus will God bring with him.

15 For this we say unto you by the word of the Lord, that we which are alive and remain unto the coming of the Lord shall not prevent [precede] them which are asleep.

16 For the Lord himself shall descend from heaven with a shout, with the voice of the archangel, and with the trump [trumpet call] of God: and the dead in Christ shall rise first:

17 Then we which are alive and remain shall be caught up together with them in the clouds, to meet the Lord in the air: and so shall we ever be with the Lord.

18 Wherefore comfort one another with these words.

Chapter 5

1 But of the times and the seasons, brethren, ye have no need that I write unto you.

2 For yourselves know perfectly that the **day of the Lord** so cometh as a thief in the night.

3 For when they shall say, Peace and safety; then sudden destruction cometh upon them, as travail upon a woman with child; and they shall not escape.

4 But ye, brethren, are not in darkness, that that day should overtake you as a thief.

9 For God hath not appointed us to wrath, but to obtain salvation by our Lord Jesus Christ,

10 Who died for us, that, whether we wake or sleep, we should live together with him.

❐ Pretending the man-made chapter break doesn't exist, read 1 Thessalonians 4:17–5:3, and then answer these questions: Will the servants of Christ be raptured (caught up to meet Jesus) on the Day of the Lord (4:17 and 5:2)? _________________ Will sudden destruction come upon sinners on the Day of the Lord (5:2–3)? _________

❐ When we studied 2 Thessalonians 1:6–2:12 in section 1, did we learn that believers will be gathered (raptured) on the Day of the Lord? _________ Did we learn that sinners will be destroyed on the Day of the Lord? _________

❐ Therefore, both the first and second books of Thessalonians teach the same thing: When Jesus comes on the Day of the Lord, his followers will raptured and sinners destroyed. The fact that sinners are destroyed on this day indicates that the rapture will take place at the end of the age—not years prior to the end. ❏ True ❏ False

Note: Are you curious about what 1 Thessalonians 5:9 has to say? Read chapter 1 to learn when this wrath be poured out.

A Word of Encouragement

He [the beast] will speak against the Most High and oppress his saints and try to change the set times and the laws. The saints will be handed over to him for a time, times, and half a time [3.5 years]. But the court will sit, and his power will be taken away and completely destroyed forever. Then the sovereignty, power and greatness of the kingdoms under the whole heaven will be handed over to the saints, the people of the Most High. His kingdom will be an everlasting kingdom, and all rulers will worship and obey him. (Daniel 7:25–27)

Section 3

We will see in this section that the Day of the Lord and the Great Tribulation are separate and distinct periods of time. The Day of the Lord will come directly **after** the Great Tribulation. The Great Tribulation is the time of the persecution of the saints who refuse to worship the beast, and the Day of the Lord is the time of the rapture of the saints still alive and the destruction of sinners.

Why do we have to investigate this? Because pre-tribulation teachers (at least some of them) believe and teach that the Day of the Lord spans a period of seven years and is also referred to as the Great Tribulation. They teach that it is during this time that the Lord will pour out his wrath. If the Great Tribulation was the wrath of God rather than the fury of Satan, they would possibly be right in saying that the rapture must take place before the start of the Great Tribulation because 1 Thessalonians 5:9 says believers will not suffer the wrath of God. But as we learned in chapter 1, the Great Tribulation is a time of Satan's fury, not the time of God's *Strong's* G3709 wrath. (To learn why I think pre-tribulationists teach this, go to chapter 12, section 7).

Now I don't expect you to believe that the Day of the Lord is distinct from the Great Tribulation just because I do. I want you to believe it because Scripture teaches it, so let's look into it.

Before we get started, please recall something we learned in a previous chapter: The Great and Dreadful Day of the Lord, the Great Day of His Wrath, and the Day of the Lord are different names for the same day.

Let's study the three passages below—which can be easily linked together because of the mention of a darkened sun and moon and falling stars—to help us determine whether or not the Great Tribulation is the Day of the Lord.

Read the following passages, carefully observing the emphasized words to see why we are linking the passages together:

[Jesus said,] "Immediately after the tribulation of those days **the sun will be darkened, and the moon will not give its light; the stars will fall from heaven**, and the powers of the heavens will be shaken. Then the sign of the Son of Man will appear in heaven and then all the tribes of the earth will mourn, and they will see the Son of Man coming on the clouds of heaven with power and great glory. And He will send His angels with a great sound of a trumpet, and they will gather together His elect from the four winds, from one end of heaven to the other." (Matthew 24:29–31, NKJV)

The **sun will be turned to darkness and the moon to blood** *before* the coming of the great and dreadful day of the Lord. (Joel 2:31)

And I beheld when he had opened the sixth seal, and, lo, there was a great earthquake; and **the sun became black as sackcloth of hair, and the moon became as blood; And the stars of heaven fell unto the earth**, even as a fig tree casteth her untimely figs, when she is shaken of a mighty wind. And the heaven [sky] departed as a scroll when it is rolled together; and every mountain and island were moved out of their places. And the kings of the earth, and the great men, and the rich men, and the chief captains, and the mighty men, and every bondman, and every free man, hid themselves in the dens and in the rocks of the mountains; And said to the mountains and rocks, Fall on us, and hide us from the

> face of him that sitteth on the throne, and from
> the wrath of the Lamb: For the great day of his
> wrath is come; and who shall be able to stand?
> (Revelation 6:12–17, KJV)

Now we need to look at the chronology taught in each of the passages above.

❏ Does Matthew 24:29–31 teach the following sequential order? ___________

- The tribulation of those days (known as the Great Tribulation) will take place.

- The sun and the moon will go dark, and the stars will fall from heaven.

- Jesus will return in the clouds.

❏ Does Joel 2:31 teach the following sequential order? ___________

- The sun will turn to darkness and the moon to blood.

- The Great and Dreadful Day of the Lord, aka the Day of the Lord, will occur.

❏ Does Revelation 6:12–17 teach the following sequential order? ___________

- The sun will turn black, the moon will turn blood red, and the stars will fall from heaven.

- The Great Day of His Wrath, aka the Day of the Lord, will occur.

Mark the following evidence true or false.

- ❐ The evidence in the Matthew 24 passage shows that the Great Tribulation will occur **before** the sun and the moon go dark and the stars fall from heaven. ❏ True ❏ False

- ❐ The evidence in the Joel 2 passage reveals that the Great and Dreadful Day of the Lord (aka the Day of the Lord) will occur **after** the sun and the moon go dark and the stars fall from the sky. ❏ True ❏ False

- ❐ According to the Revelation 6 passage, the Great Day of His Wrath (aka the Day of the Lord) will occur **after** the sun and the moon go dark and the stars fall from heaven. ❏ True ❏ False

Now answer this:

- ❐ Since the Great Tribulation occurs **before** the sun and the moon go dark and the stars fall from heaven, and the Day of the Lord occurs **after** the sun and the moon go dark and the stars from heaven, they must be separate and distinct periods of time. ❏ True ❏ False

Let's examine Zephaniah 1:14–18 and 2 Peter 3:10–14 to see if the Day of the Lord could come any earlier than the last day of the age.

Here is the Zephaniah passage:

> The **great day of the Lord** is near, it is near, and hasteth greatly, even the voice of the **day of the Lord:** the mighty man shall cry there bitterly. That day is a day of wrath, a day of trouble and distress, a day of wasteness and desolation, a day of darkness and gloominess, a day of clouds and thick darkness, a day of the trumpet and alarm against the fenced cities, and against the high

> towers. And I will bring distress upon men, that they shall walk like blind men, because they have sinned against the Lord: and their blood shall be poured out as dust, and their flesh as the dung. Neither their silver nor their gold shall be able to deliver them in the **day of the Lord's wrath**; but the whole land shall be devoured by the fire of his jealousy: for he shall make even a speedy riddance of all them that dwell in the land. (Zephaniah 1:14–18, KJV)

❏ According to the last verse in the passage above, what will take place on the Day of the Lord and what are two other names for that day?

Here is the 2 Peter 3:10–14 passage:

> But the **day of the Lord** will come as a thief in the night; in which the heavens shall pass away with a great noise, and the elements shall melt with fervent heat, the earth also and the works that are therein shall be burned up. Seeing then that all these things shall be dissolved, what manner of persons ought ye to be in all holy conversation and godliness, looking for and hasting unto the coming of the **day of God,** wherein the heavens being on fire shall be dissolved, and the elements shall melt with fervent heat? Nevertheless we, according to his promise, look for new heavens and a new earth, wherein dwelleth righteousness. Wherefore, beloved, seeing that ye look for such

> things, be diligent that ye may be found of him in peace, without spot, and blameless. (2 Peter 3:10–14, KJV)

❏ According to the 2 Peter 3 passage above, what will happen on the Day of the Lord (aka the Day of God)?

❏ We just looked at two Day of the Lord passages (Zephaniah 1:14-18 and 2 Peter 3:10-14). If the things that are mentioned in those two passages take place on the Day of the Lord, there is no way that day could come any earlier than the very end. ❏ True ❏ False

Let's think about what Revelation 13, Matthew 24, Daniel 7, and 2 Thessalonians 2 tell us about what will take place during the Great Tribulation. Since we learned about these things previously, this will just be a summary:

> The beast will seat himself in the temple of God. He will have authority over all who live on the face of the earth for forty-two months. The people of the earth (except God's people) will take the mark of the beast and worship him so they can continue to buy and sell. Those who refuse to worship the beast will be persecuted.

❏ With that said, answer this: Does the Great Tribulation, the time of the **persecution of the saints**, seem like the same period of time as the Day of the Lord, the time of the **destruction of the earth and the sinners therein**? ___________

❏ According to 2 Peter 3:12 in the NIV, believers look forward to this day, the day of the destruction of the earth and its sinners. (That seems odd, doesn't it?) Why would we want this day to come? Because "we are looking forward to a new heaven and a new earth, where righteousness dwells" (2 Peter 3:13, NIV). ❏ True ❏ False

❏ There are many other reasons to look forward to the Day of the Lord. Besides being raptured and/or resurrected, here are two more of them. (Check the box after you have read them.)

> Dear friends, now we are children of God, and what we will be has not yet been made known. But we know that when he appears, we shall be like him, for we shall see him as he is. (1 John 3:2)

> Now there is in store for me the crown of righteousness, which the Lord, the righteous Judge, will award to me on that day—and not only to me, but also to all who have longed for his appearing. (2 Timothy 4:8)

Mark whether the following statements are true or false:

❏ On the Day of the Lord, the Lord will return, destroy sinners, destroy the man of lawlessness, and destroy the heavens and the earth, after which there will be a new heaven and a new earth—a new age. The Lord will rapture us on this day, just before the sinners and the beast are destroyed. ❏ True ❏ False

❏ The Great Tribulation and the Day of the Lord are separate and distinct periods of time. ❏ True ❏ False

Record here anything that you disagree with or are not sure about:

____

____

____

____

____

____

Chapter 7
The Day Lot Left Sodom

Now let's turn our attention to the day Lot left Sodom. We shall see that Lot was rescued out of the city **just before** the people of Sodom were destroyed (Genesis 19:1–29). Why are we studying that day? Because Jesus said the day the Son of Man is going to be revealed will be just like the day Lot left Sodom:

> [Jesus said,] "People were eating and drinking, buying and selling, planting and building. But the day Lot left Sodom, fire and sulfur rained down from heaven and destroyed them all. **It will be just like this on the day the Son of Man is revealed**… I tell you, on that night two people will be in one bed; **one will be taken and the other left**. Two women will be grinding grain together; **one will be taken and the other left**."
> (Luke 17:28–30, 34–35)

If the day that the Son of Man is going to be revealed will be like the day Lot was rescued from Sodom, then could it be that those who are taken are those who will be raptured and that they will be raptured **on the same day** that the people of the world are destroyed? Let's see if Scripture bears this out.

Read the two main passages below before moving on to the questions.

Luke 17:22-35

22 [Jesus said to his <u>disciples</u>,] "The time is coming when you will <u>long</u> to see <u>one</u> of the days of the Son of Man, but you will not see <u>it</u>.
23 "Men will tell you, 'There he is!' or 'Here he is!' Do not go running off after them.
24 "For the Son of Man in his day will be like the lightning, which flashes and lights up the sky from one end to the other.
25 "But first he must suffer many things and be rejected by this generation.
26 "Just as it was in the days of Noah, so also will it be in the days of the Son of Man.
27 "People were eating, drinking, marrying and being given in marriage up to the day Noah entered the ark. Then the flood came and destroyed them all.
28 "It was the same in the days of Lot. People were eating and drinking, buying and selling, planting and building.
29 "But the day Lot left Sodom, fire and sulfur rained down from heaven and destroyed them all.
30 "It will be just like this on the day the Son of Man is revealed.
31 "On that day no one who is on the roof of his house, with his goods inside, should go down to get them. Likewise, no one in the field should go back for anything.
32 "Remember Lot's wife!
33 "Whoever tries to keep his life will lose it, and whoever loses his life will preserve it.

34 "I tell you, on that night two people will be in one bed; one will be taken and the other left.
35 "Two women will be grinding grain together; one will be taken and the other left."

Matthew 24:15-16, 21-22, 29-31, 40-42 (NKJV)

15 [Jesus said,] "Therefore when you see the 'abomination of desolation,' spoken of by Daniel the prophet, standing in the holy place (whoever reads, let him understand),
16 "then let those who are in Judea flee to the mountains.

21 "For then [when we see the abomination of desolation] there will be Great Tribulation, such as has not been since the beginning of the world until this time, no, nor ever shall be.
22 And unless those days were shortened, no flesh would be saved; but for the elect's sake those days will be shortened.

29 "Immediately after the tribulation of those days the sun will be darkened, and the moon will not give its light; the stars will fall from heaven, and the powers of the heavens will be shaken.
30 "Then the sign of the Son of Man will appear in heaven and then all the tribes of the earth will mourn, and they will see the Son of Man coming on the clouds of heaven with power and great glory.
31 "And He will send His angels with a great sound of a trumpet, and they will gather together His elect from the four winds, from one end of heaven to the other.

40 "Then two men will be in the field: one will be taken and the other left.
41 "Two women will be grinding at the mill: one will be taken and the other left.
42 "Watch therefore, for you do not know what hour your Lord is coming."

First, let's study the Luke 17 passage. Before we study what we see in the passage, let's take note of what we do **not** see. Jesus, talking to his disciples (members of the Lord's body, just as we are), told them there would come a time when they would "long to see one of the days of the Son of Man" (verse 22). But he made no mention of a pre-tribulation rapture. Allow that to sink in. Could it be because our blessed hope is not escape from tribulation but the appearing of our great God and Savior, Jesus Christ (Titus 2:13)?

Now let's learn about what we **do** see in the Luke 17 passage by hyperfocusing on the details.

❏ According to verse 22, Jesus was talking to his ___________ ___________________.

❏ Verse 22 says, "The time is coming when you will _____________________ to see ___________ of the days of the Son of Man, but you will not see _______."

❏ How many days did the disciples long to see?
❏ One ❏ More than one

❏ Will the happenings listed below take place **on the one day** that will be like the day Lot left Sodom (verses 29–30)? ___________ Is this the day believers long to see? ___________

- The Son of Man (Jesus) will be revealed (verse 30).

- He will light up the sky from one end to the other (verse 24).

- Some will be taken (verses 34–35).

Who will be taken? Who will be left? Let's study hard to find the answers.

To start with, we'll compare the Genesis account with our Luke 17 passage. Read the summary of Genesis 19:1–29 below, a summary of the day Lot left Sodom. (If you wish to read the entire account, read Genesis 18:16 through 19:29 *in your Bible*.)

> Sodom was about to be destroyed; but before it was, the Lord, because he was merciful, sent two angels to lead Lot and his family safely out of the city. One of the angels said to him, "The outcry to the Lord against its people is so great that he has sent us to destroy it."
>
> The angels took the hands of Lot, his wife, and his two daughters and led them out of Sodom. One of the angels said to them, "Flee for your lives! Don't look back, and don't stop anywhere in the plain! Flee to the mountains or you will be swept away!"
>
> When Lot asked if they could flee to Zoar, one of the angels said, "Flee there quickly, because I cannot do anything until you reach it. (That is why the town was called Zoar.) By the time Lot reached Zoar, the sun had risen over the land. Then the Lord rained down burning sulfur on Sodom and Gomorrah—from the Lord out of the heavens."
>
> "But Lot's wife looked back, and she became a pillar of salt."

Let's look at some of the ways that the day the revealing of the Son of Man will be like the day Lot went out from Sodom. Check them off as you go.

❏ Comparison no. 1

- According to Genesis 19:17, Lot and his family were told, "Flee for your lives. Don't look back."

- According to Luke 17:31, Jesus said to his disciples, "No one in the field should go back for anything."

❏ Comparison no. 2

- Genesis 19:26 states, "Lot's wife looked back, and she became a pillar of salt."

- According to Luke 17:32–33, we are to "remember Lot's wife! Whoever tries to keep his life will lose it."

❏ Comparison no. 3

- According to the Genesis 19:16, Lot and the others were taken out of Sodom by the angels.

- According to Luke 17:34, "One will be taken..."

With the Genesis story and the comparisons in mind, read Luke 17:29–35, and then answer these questions:

❏ Was the life of Lot's wife, who wanted to go back to Sodom, lost? __________ Was she turned into salt? __________ According to the second paragraph of the summary of the Genesis story, did the Lord desire to save her? __________

❏ Was the life of Lot, who was willing to give up everything he had in Sodom and be taken out of the city, spared? __________

❏ Does the passage below help you understand what Jesus meant by saying what he did in Luke 17:33? ___________

> Then Jesus said to His disciples, "If anyone wants to come after Me, he must deny himself, take up his cross, and follow Me. For whoever wants to save his life will lose it; but whoever loses his life for My sake will find it. For what good will it do a person if he gains the whole world, but forfeits his soul? Or what will a person give in exchange for his soul?" (Matthew 16:24–26)

Now remembering that Jesus said we should remember Lot's wife (verse 32) just before he said, "Whoever tries to keep his life will lose it, and whoever loses his life will preserve it" (verse 33), answer these questions:

❏ Do you think the ones who, like Lot's wife, want to keep their lives are the ones who will be left (verses 34–35) and will thus lose their lives (verse 33)? ___________

❏ Do you think that the ones who, like Lot, are willing to lose their lives are the ones who will be taken? ___________

❏ If the angels came to bring you to Jesus, would you want them to take you, or would you want to keep living for what the world has to offer? ___________

❏ Second Peter 3:7 says the present earth and ungodly people will be destroyed by fire. The people of Sodom were destroyed by fire and sulfur. Do you think that may mean that those who are left (Luke 17:34–35) will be destroyed by fire?___________

❏ Does Luke 17:29 tell us that **on the very same day** Lot was taken out of Sodom the residents of Sodom were destroyed? ___________ And does Luke 17:30 say, "It will be just like this on the day the Son of Man is revealed"? ___________ Since the day that the Son of Man will be revealed will be just like the day Lot was taken out of Sodom, it seems likely that the rescue of some and the destruction of others will take place **on the same day.** ❑ True ❑ False

❑ If the ones who are taken are the ones who will be raptured, then the rapture will take place on the last day of the age, the day of the destruction of all the unsaved people in the world. ❑ True ❑ False

❑ According to the verses below, if someone isn't saved, is it God's fault? __________

> He [God] is patient with you, not wanting anyone to perish, but everyone to come to repentance. (2 Peter 3:9)

> [God] commandeth all men everywhere to repent [turn away from their sins toward him]. (Acts 17:30, KJV)

> They perish because they refused to love the truth and so be saved. For this reason God sends them a powerful delusion so that they will believe the lie and so that all will be condemned who have not believed the truth but have delighted in wickedness. (2 Thessalonians 2:10–12)

> [Jesus said,] O Jerusalem, Jerusalem, thou that killest the prophets, and stonest them which are sent unto thee, how often would I have gathered thy children together, even as a hen gathereth her chickens under her wings, and ye would not! (Matthew 23:37, KJV)

> Whoever is thirsty, let him come; and whoever
> wishes, let him take the free gift of the water of
> life. (Revelation 22:17)

Second, let's turn our attention to the Matthew passage, which also contains the verses that say one will be taken and one will be left (Matthew 24:40–41).

❏ Because the Luke 17 and Matthew 24 passages are speaking of the same period of time, Luke 17:34–35 and Matthew 24:40–41 must both be referring to the same happenings.
❏ True ❏ False

Read Matthew 24:30–31 and 40–42 a couple of times over so that the context of verses 40 and 41 becomes apparent, and then answer the questions that follow:

❏ Does verse 30 speak of Jesus's coming? ___________

❏ Does verse 42 speak of Jesus's coming? ___________

❏ Are verses 30 and 42 speaking of the same coming? ___________

❏ Read verses 30–31. Do they say that angels will gather the elect when Jesus comes? ___________

❏ Do verses 40–42 say that some will be taken when Jesus comes? ___________ Does it seem to you that the ones who will be taken are the ones who will be gathered? ___________

❏ Verse 42 (NKJV) reads, "Watch therefore, for you do not know what hour **your** Lord is coming." The reader, whose Lord is Jesus, is being told by Jesus to watch for his coming, right?
❏ Right ❏ Wrong

Third, now that we have considered the possibility that the ones who will be taken are the ones who will be gathered by the angels, let's see if the gathering is the rapture. Then we'll see if the gathering will take place after the reign of the beast, the time of the Great Tribulation.

Look at the two passages below, and then answer the questions that follow.

> [Jesus said,] "At that time the sign of the Son of Man will appear in the sky, and all the nations of the earth will mourn. They will see the Son of Man **coming** on the clouds of the sky, with power and great glory. And he will send his angels with a loud trumpet call, and they will **gather** his elect from the four winds, from one end of the heavens to the other." (Matthew 24:30–31)

> Concerning the **coming** of our Lord Jesus Christ and our being **gathered** to him, we ask you, brothers, not to become easily unsettled or alarmed by some prophecy, report, or letter supposed to have come from us, saying that the Day of the Lord has already come. (2 Thessalonians 2:1–2)

❏ Do both passages speak of the **coming** of the Lord? ____________

❏ Do both passages speak of the **gathering** of the saints at the coming of Jesus? ____________

❏ If the 2 Thessalonians passage pertains to the coming of Jesus and the rapture, then is it likely that Matthew 24:30–31 does also? ____________

Read 2 Thessalonians 2:1–8 *in your Bible*, and then answer these questions:

❏ According to verse 1, will a gathering of the saints take place when Jesus comes? ____________

- ❏ According to verses 1–3, will the coming of our Lord and our being gathered to him come before or after the man of lawlessness is revealed? ❏ Before ❏ After

- ❏ Read verse 8, and then answer this question: Will the lawless one be destroyed **when Jesus comes**? ___________ Now read verse 1 again, and then answer this question: will believers be gathered **when Jesus comes**? ___________

- ❏ According to verses 1–8, the gathering (rapture) will take place **after** the reign of the lawless one, which will begin at his revealing when he stands in the temple claiming to be God and will end when Jesus destroys him. ❏ True ❏ False

Now read Daniel 7:25–26 *in your Bible.* Considering this passage and 2 Thessalonians 2:1–8, answer these questions:

- ❏ According to Daniel 7:25–26, will the power of the beast (the lawless one) be destroyed **after** his reign of 3.5 years (a time, times, and half a time), the period during which the saints are handed over to him? ___________

- ❏ If the power of the lawless one is destroyed after his 3.5-year reign and we are gathered on that day, will we be gathered at the end of his reign rather than years before his reign? ___________

- ❏ Does the fact that we are persecuted by the beast during his reign of a time, times, and a half a time (3.5 years) and we are gathered to the Lord when his reign comes to an end eliminate any possibility that the gathering (rapture) could take place **before** the man of lawlessness (the abomination of desolation) stands in the temple claiming to be God at the beginning of his reign? ___________

Read Matthew 24:15, 21, 29–31, and then answer the following questions:

- ☐ Would you say that the angels gather the elect **after** the abomination of desolation stands in the holy place (the temple) and **after** the tribulation of those days (the Great Tribulation)? _______

- ☐ Does that eliminate the possibility that the gathering will take place before the time of great tribulation? _______

Let's put it together.

- ☐ Second Thessalonians 2:1 is most definitely a rapture verse. It speaks of the coming of Jesus and the gathering of the saints at his coming. We learned that this **gathering** will occur after the reign of the lawless one. Matthew 24:29–31 says the elect will be **gathered** at the coming of the Lord Jesus after the tribulation of those days—the time of the reign of the abomination of desolation (aka the beast, the lawless one). Putting these pieces of the puzzle in their proper places, we learn that the rapture will be a post-tribulation event. ☐ True ☐ False

Check the statements you agree with:

- ☐ Lot was taken out of Sodom just before the people of Sodom were destroyed. It will be like this when Jesus is revealed.

- ☐ The elect will be taken after the abomination of desolation stands in the temple and after the Great Tribulation (the time of persecution of the saints), at the end of the age.

Record here anything that you disagree with or are not sure about:

____

____

____

____

____

____

Chapter 8

A Thief Is Coming!

The saints will be gathered to Jesus when he comes like a thief. Just as one doesn't know when a thief will come, we won't know when Jesus, our master, will come; he might come anytime during the "evening, or at midnight, or when a rooster crows, or at dawn" (Mark 13:35). Will this gathering take place at the end of the age when Jesus comes to destroy the heavens and the earth and its unforgiven sinners, or will it take place years earlier than that? We need to find out.

You have already studied the passages below—more than once—but now we are going to look at them from yet another angle: We will see how the thief references link these passages together, and we'll see what that tells us about the timing of the rapture.

---

1 Thessalonians 4:16-5:4 (KJV)

Chapter 4
16 For the Lord himself shall descend from heaven with a shout, with the voice of the archangel, and with the trump [trumpet call] of God: and the dead in Christ shall rise first:
17 Then we which are alive and remain shall be caught up together with them in the clouds, to meet the Lord in the air: and so shall we ever be with the Lord.
18 Wherefore comfort one another with these words.

Chapter 5
1 But of the times and the seasons, brethren, ye have no need that I write unto you.
2 For yourselves know perfectly that the day of the Lord so cometh as a **thief** in the night.
3 For when they shall say, Peace and safety; then sudden destruction cometh upon them, as travail upon a woman with child; and they shall not escape.
4 But ye, brethren, are not in darkness, that that day should overtake you as a **thief**.

Peter 3:10-13 (KJV)

10 But the day of the Lord will come as a **thief** in the night; in which the heavens shall pass away with a great noise, and the elements shall melt with fervent heat, the earth also and the works that are therein shall be burned up.
11 Seeing then that all these things shall be dissolved, what manner of persons ought ye to be in all holy conversation and godliness,
12 Looking for and hasting unto the coming of the day of God, wherein the heavens being on fire shall be dissolved, and the elements shall melt with fervent heat!
13 Nevertheless we, according to his promise, look for new heavens and a new earth, wherein dwelleth righteousness.

Revelation 16:14-21 (KJV)

14 For they are the spirits of devils, working miracles, which go forth unto the kings of the earth and of the whole world, to gather them to the battle of that great day of God Almighty.

15 Behold, I [Jesus] come as a **thief**. Blessed is he that watcheth, and keepeth his garments, lest he walk naked, and they see his shame.

16 And he gathered them together into a place called in the Hebrew tongue Armageddon.

17 And the seventh angel poured out his vial into the air; and there came a great voice out of the temple of heaven, from the throne, saying, It is done.

18 And there were voices, and thunders, and lightnings; and there was a great earthquake, such as was not since men were upon the earth, so mighty an earthquake, and so great.

19 And the great city was divided into three parts, and the cities of the nations fell: and great Babylon came in remembrance before God, to give unto her the cup of the wine of the fierceness of his wrath.

20 And every island fled away, and the mountains were not found.

21 And there fell upon men a great hail out of heaven, every stone about the weight of a talent: and men blasphemed God because of the plague of the hail; for the plague thereof was exceeding great.

First, let's explore the 1 Thessalonians passage. Read the passage, ignoring the man-made chapter break, and focus on 1 Thessalonians 4:17 and 5:2–3. Now answer these questions:

- According to 4:17 and 5:2, will we be raptured (caught up) to meet Jesus when he comes on the Day of the Lord that will come like a thief in the night? __________

- According to 5:2–3, will sudden destruction come upon unbelievers on the Day of the Lord that will come like a thief in the night? __________

So that you can confirm what we just saw in the 1 Thessalonians passage, turn to 2 Thessalonians *in your Bible.*

❏ According to 2 Thessalonians 1:9–10 and 2:1–2, will we be raptured **and** sinners punished with everlasting destruction when Jesus comes on the Day of the Lord? _________ Therefore, do those verses confirm what the 1 Thessalonians passage teaches: The rapture and the destruction of sinners will occur on the Day of the Lord, which, according to 1 Thessalonians 5:2, will come like a thief in the night? _________

❏ One more thing: according to 2 Thessalonians 2:8, will the lawless one be destroyed on the same day, the day Jesus comes? _________

❏ Does the fact that unbelievers will be suddenly destroyed and the lawless one overthrown on this day reveal that the day that will come like a thief in the night will not occur until the end of the age? _________ Since the rapture will take place on that same day, the rapture will not take place until the end of the age. ❏ True ❏ False

Second, we'll examine and link together the 2 Peter passage and the 1 Thessalonians passage to see what that tells us.

❏ Just as 1 Thessalonians 5:2 refers to the day we are studying as the Day of the Lord and says it will come like a thief in the night, so does 2 Peter 3:10, and the wording is almost the same. Read the verses below. Then compare the wording. Then answer this question: does it seem both passages must be referring to the same day? _________

> The day of the Lord so comes as a thief in the night. (1 Thessalonians 5:2)

> But the day of the Lord will come like a thief in the night. (2 Peter 3:10)

❏ Read 2 Peter 3:10–13. What statements in that passage indicate that the Day of the Lord that "will come like a thief in the night" will occur at the end of the current age and the beginning of a new age?

❏ Therefore, linking the 2 Peter 3 passage and the 1 Thessalonians passage teach that us that the Day of the Lord will come like a thief in the night at the end of the age (not seven or so years before that), and the 1 Thessalonians passage tells us that we will be raptured on that day. ❏ True ❏ False

Third, now let's examine and link together the Revelation 16 passage and the 1 Thessalonians passage to see what that reveals.

❏ Revelation 16:14–16 addresses the point in time that believers are to watch for the return of Christ, who will come like a thief: it is just before the kings of the earth of the whole world are gathered to a place called Armageddon. ❏ True ❏ False

❏ What does it say in Revelation 16:19–20 that indicates the Lord's coming like a thief will take place at the end of the age?

❏ Did we learn from the 1 Thessalonians passage that believers will be caught up to meet Jesus in the air (raptured) on the Day of the Lord that will come like a thief in the night? ___________ When we link the 1 Thessalonians passage and the Revelation 16 passage together, we see even more evidence that believers will be raptured at the end of the age, a day that Jesus and the Day of the Lord will come like a thief. ❏ True ❏ False

Check the statements you agree with:

- ❏ According to the 1 Thessalonians passage, the Day of the Lord will come like a thief in the night, Jesus will return, believers will be raptured, and sinners will be destroyed.

- ❏ Second Thessalonians 1:9–2:8 confirms that the rapture and the destruction of sinners will take place on the Day of the Lord. It adds that the lawless one will be destroyed on that day.

- ❏ Linking the 1 Thessalonians 4 and 5 passage with the 2 Peter 3 passage reveals this: The Day of the Lord will come like a thief in the night, we will be raptured, and the earth will be burned up, after which there will be new heavens and a new earth.

- ❏ According to the Revelation 16 passage, Jesus tells believers to stay awake because he is about to come like a thief. Cities of the nations will collapse, islands will flee, and the mountains will disappear.

- ❏ The happenings that will take place in these thief passages reveal that the rapture will take place at the end of the age, not seven years or so before then.

Record here anything that you disagree with or are not sure about:

____

____

____

____

____

Chapter 9

The Appearance

In this chapter, an end-of-the-age rapture will be proven by looking at the *appearance* passages. Is there just one appearance of Jesus yet to come, or are there two appearances yet to come? Let's find out.

Note that each of the main passages contains the word *appear*, *appears*, *appearing*, or *appearance*. They are in bold typeface so that you can spot them easier.

---

2 Thessalonians 2:1-4, 8 (NASB)

1 Now we request you, brethren, with regard to the coming of our Lord Jesus Christ and our gathering together to Him,
2 that you not be quickly shaken from your composure or be disturbed either by a spirit or a message or a letter as if from us, to the effect that the day of the Lord has come.
3 Let no one in any way deceive you, for it will not come unless the apostasy comes first, and the man of lawlessness is revealed, the son of destruction
4 who opposes and exalts himself above every so-called god or object of worship, so that he takes his seat in the temple of God, displaying himself as being God.

8 Then that lawless one will be revealed whom the Lord will slay with the breath of His mouth and bring to an end by the **appearance** [G2015] of His coming.

Titus 2:11-14

11 For the grace of God that brings salvation has appeared to all men.
12 It teaches us to say "No" to ungodliness and worldly passions, and to live self-controlled, upright and godly lives in this present age,
13 while we wait for the blessed hope—the glorious **appearing** [G2015] of our great God and Savior, Jesus Christ,
14 who gave himself for us to redeem us from all wickedness and to purify for himself a people that are his very own, eager to do what is good.

---

1 John 3:2

2 Dear friends, now we are children of God, and what we will be has not yet been made known. But we know that when he **appears**, we shall be <u>like</u> him, for we shall see him as he is.

Hebrews 9:27-28

27 Just as man is destined to die once, and after that to face judgment,
28 so Christ was sacrificed once to take away the sins of many people; and he will **appear** a <u>second</u> time, not to bear sin, but to bring salvation to those who are <u>waiting</u> for him.

First, let's see what the 2 Thessalonians 2 passage reveals, and then see what we can learn by linking it to the Titus passage:

❒ According to 2 Thessalonians 2:8, will Jesus bring an end to the lawless one "by the **appearance of His coming**." __________ According to this verse, is the Lord's **coming** the <u>same event</u> as his **appearing**? __________

❒ Does 2 Thessalonians 2:1 also speak of Jesus's coming? __________ Is it at this time that believers will be gathered to him? __________ (Other chapters show that the gathering is the rapture.)

❒ Therefore, believers will be gathered/raptured **and** the lawless one destroyed at the **appearance** of Jesus's coming. ❑ True ❑ False

❒ According to Titus 2:13, is the blessed hope the glorious **appearing** of our great God and Savior, Jesus Christ? __________

❒ Does Titus 2:13 say that the blessed hope is escape from persecution? __________ (If you answered yes, I must ask: does the verse really say that, or did you read that into the verse because of what you have been taught?)

❒ To the one who endures to the end of the 3.5 years of persecution, will our Lord's **appearing** seem beyond-description glorious? __________

❒ Would you consider the coming of Jesus and the kingdom of God to be **infinitely** more of a blessed hope for the believer than escape from persecution? __________

Let's find out some other things that will make his appearance a blessed hope, as Titus 2:13 says:

- ❐ According to 1 John 3:2, when Jesus **appears**, "we shall be ______________ him, for we shall see him as he is."

- ❐ According to Hebrews 9:27–28, Jesus "will **appear** a ____________________ time, not to bear sin, but to bring salvation to those who are ____________________ for him."

Second, let's look at the 2 Timothy 4 passage and compare it to 2 Thessalonians 2: 1 and 8:

- ❐ Does 2 Timothy 4:1 seem to imply that Jesus will judge the dead when he **appears** to set up his kingdom? __________

To back this up with another passage, we shall look to this passage from the Book of Revelation:

> The seventh angel sounded his trumpet, and there were loud voices in heaven, which said: **"The kingdom of the world has become the kingdom of our Lord and of his Christ**, and he will reign for ever and ever." And the twenty-four elders, who were seated on their thrones before God, fell on their faces and worshiped God, saying: "We give thanks to you, Lord God Almighty, the One who is and who was, because you have taken your great power and have begun to reign. The nations were angry; and your wrath has come. **The time has come for judging the dead**, and for rewarding your servants the prophets and your saints and those who reverence your name, both small and great—and for destroying those who destroy the earth." (Revelation 11:15–18)

❑ Does the passage above make clear that Jesus will judge the dead **when** the kingdom of the world becomes the kingdom of our Lord and of his Christ? ___________

❑ So then, Jesus's **appearing** will take place when he comes to set up his kingdom. ❑ True ❑ False

❑ If Jesus's appearing takes place when he comes to set up his kingdom and we are gathered to him when he comes/**appears**, we won't be gathered/raptured until the end of the age and the beginning of the new age (the thousand-year reign of Jesus). ❑ True ❑ False

Third, let's see if Jesus will come out of heaven for a pre-tribulation rapture before he comes to set up his kingdom.

❑ Read the following two passages (Acts 1:6–8 and Acts 3:21 below), paying attention to what Jesus will restore, and then answer this question: will Jesus come out of heaven for anything at all before it is time to set up his kingdom? ___________

> So when they [the Lord's followers] met together [before Jesus rose into heaven], they asked him, "Lord, are you at this time going to restore the kingdom to Israel?" He said to them: "It is not for you to know the times or dates the Father has set by his own authority. But you will receive power when the Holy Spirit comes on you; and you will be my witnesses in Jerusalem, and in all Judea and Samaria, and to the ends of the earth." (Acts 1:6–8)

> He [Jesus] must remain in heaven until the time comes for God to restore everything, as he promised long ago through his holy prophets. (Acts 3:21)

☐ If Jesus won't come out of heaven until it is time to restore the kingdom to Israel, will he come out of heaven to rapture his saints seven or so years before the end of the kingdom of the world and the beginning of the kingdom of our Lord?

It thoroughly grieves me that the blessed hope is seen by many as an escape from persecution rather than the wonder of all that will take place when Jesus comes to set up his kingdom. "For our light and momentary troubles are achieving for us an eternal glory that far outweighs them all" (2 Corinthians 4:17). When Jesus returns, he will reign as king over the world, we will be brought together with those who have died in the Lord, we will be with him forever, we will never sin again. Sinners and the beast will be destroyed, and the earth will be the home of righteousness. Will a short time of persecution not seem like a light and momentary trouble compared to the glory in store for us?

The teaching that the blessed hope is an escape from persecution is an especially grievous teaching since Scripture says we are destined for persecution and that great blessings come to those who are persecuted for his name's sake. (See chapter 11 to learn more about that.)

Check the statements you agree with:

☐ Jesus must remain in heaven until it is time to restore the kingdom (Acts 1:6–8 and 3:21).

☐ Jesus, when it is time to set up his kingdom, will <u>appear</u> (2 Timothy 4:1).

☐ Saints are waiting for the blessed hope—the glorious <u>appearing</u> of Jesus Christ (Titus 2:13).

☐ Believers will be gathered to Jesus and the lawless one brought to an end when Jesus comes/<u>appears</u> (2 Thessalonians 2:1, 8).

☐ Jesus will bring us salvation and make us like him when he <u>appears</u> (1 John 3:2 and Hebrews 9:27–28).

☐ Linking the passages in this chapter reveals that the rapture will not take place until Jesus <u>appears</u> at the end of the age when it is time to destroy the beast and set up his kingdom.

Record here anything that you disagree with or are not sure about:

____

____

____

____

____

____

Chapter 10
The Coming

You will find even more proof of a post-tribulation, end-of-the-age rapture by studying and linking the *coming* passages.

Matthew 24 is a *coming* passage; it depicts Jesus coming in the clouds and the angels gathering the elect. If you have studied other chapters, you already know that pre-tribulationists say the gathering mentioned in Matthew 24:31 is not the rapture. They must deny it as the rapture because they teach a pre-tribulation rapture, and Matthew 24:29–31 (see below) says this gathering will not take place until **after** the tribulation period.

> **Immediately after the tribulation** of those days, the sun will be darkened, and the moon will not give its light; the stars will fall from heaven, and the powers of the heavens will be shaken. Then the sign of the Son of Man will appear in heaven, and then all the tribes of the earth will mourn, and they will see the Son of Man coming on the clouds of heaven with power and great glory. And **He will send His angels with a great sound of a trumpet, and they will gather together His elect** from the four winds, from one end of heaven to the other. (Matthew 24:29–31, NASB)

Because the period of time before the return of Jesus is called the "times of the Gentiles" in Luke 21:24, I am going to call it the *Gentile age*. It, the current age, is an age that will end when Jesus comes in the clouds. How do I know this? The disciples asked for a sign of Jesus's coming and of the end of the age (Matthew 24:3). Then in Matthew 24:30, we see that Jesus himself is the sign. His coming in the clouds will mark the end of the current age (the Gentile age, wherein mostly Gentiles but some Jews also are being saved) and the beginning of a new age, the reign of Jesus Christ as king of the earth.

Luke 21:12-28, 34-36

12 [Jesus said,] "But before all this, they will lay hands on you and persecute you. They will deliver you to synagogues and prisons, and you will be brought before kings and governors, and all on account of my name.
13 "This will result in your being witnesses to them.
14 "But make up your mind not to worry beforehand how you will defend yourselves.
15 "For I will give you words and wisdom that none of your adversaries will be able to resist or contradict.
16 "You will be betrayed even by parents, brothers, relatives and friends, and they will put some of you to death.
17 "All men will hate you because of me.
18 "But not a hair of your head will perish.
19 "By standing firm you will gain life.
20 "When you see Jerusalem being surrounded by armies, you will know that its desolation is near.
21 "Then let those who are in Judea flee to the mountains, let those in the city get out, and let those in the country not enter the city.
22 "For this is the time of punishment in fulfillment of all that has been written.

23 "How dreadful it will be in those days for pregnant women and nursing mothers! There will be great distress in the land and wrath against this people.

24 "They will fall by the sword and will be taken as prisoners to all the nations. Jerusalem will be trampled on by the Gentiles until the times of the Gentiles are fulfilled.

25 "There will be signs in the sun, moon and stars. On the earth, nations will be in anguish and perplexity at the roaring and tossing of the sea.

26 "Men will faint from terror, apprehensive of what is coming on the world, for the heavenly bodies will be shaken.

27 "At that time they will see the Son of Man **coming** in a cloud with power and great glory.

28 "When these things begin to take place, stand up and lift up your heads, because your redemption is drawing near.

34 "Be careful, or your hearts will be weighed down with dissipation, drunkenness and the anxieties of life, and that day will close on you unexpectedly like a trap.

35 "For it will come upon all those who live on the face of the whole earth.

36 "Be always on the watch, and pray that you may be able to escape all that is about to happen, and that you may be able to stand before the Son of Man."

Matthew 24:3, 9, 13-21, 29-44 (NKJV)

3 Now as He sat on the Mount of Olives, the disciples came to Him privately, saying, "Tell us, when will these things be? And what will be the sign of Your **coming**, and of the end of the age?"

9 [Jesus said,] "Then they will deliver you up to tribulation and kill you, and you will be hated by all nations for My name's sake.

13 "But he who endures to the end shall be saved.
14 "And this gospel of the kingdom will be preached in all the world as a witness to all the nations and then the end will come.
15 "Therefore when you see the 'abomination of desolation,' spoken of by Daniel the prophet, standing in the <u>holy</u> place (whoever reads, let him understand),
16 then let those who are in Judea flee to the mountains.
17 "Let him who is on the housetop not go down to take anything out of his house.
18 "And let him who is in the field not go back to get his clothes.
19 "But woe to those who are pregnant and to those who are nursing babies in those days!
20 "And pray that your flight may not be in winter or on the Sabbath.
21 "For then [when we see the abomination of desolation] there will be great tribulation, such as has not been since the beginning of the world until this time, no, nor ever shall be.

29 "Immediately after the tribulation of those days the sun will be darkened, and the moon will not give its light; the stars will fall from heaven, and the powers of the heavens will be shaken.
30 "Then the sign of the Son of Man will appear in heaven and then all the tribes of the earth will

mourn, and they will see the Son of Man **coming** on the clouds of heaven with power and great glory.

31 "And He will send His angels with a great sound of a trumpet, and they will gather together His elect from the four winds, from one end of heaven to the other.

32 "Now learn this parable from the fig tree: When its branch has already become tender and puts forth leaves, you know that summer is near.

33 "So you also, when you see all these things, know that it is near—at the doors!

34 "Assuredly, I say to you, this generation will by no means pass away till all these things take place.

35 "Heaven and earth will pass away, but My words will by no means pass away.

36 "But of that day and hour no one knows, not even the angels of heaven, but My Father only.

37 "But as the days of Noah were, so also will the **coming** of the Son of Man be.

38 "For as in the days before the flood, they were eating and drinking, marrying and giving in marriage, until the day that Noah entered the ark,

39 and did not know until the flood came and took them all away, so also will the **coming** of the Son of Man be.

40 "Then two men will be in the field: one will be taken and the other left.

41 "Two women will be grinding at the mill: one will be taken and the other left.

42 "Watch therefore, for you do not know what hour your Lord is **coming**.

43 "But know this, that if the master of the house had known what hour the thief would come, he would have watched and not allowed his house to be broken into.

44 "Therefore you also be ready, for the Son of Man is **coming** at an hour you do not expect."

---

1 Thessalonians 4:13–5:3 (KJV)

Chapter 4

13 But I would not have you to be ignorant, brethren, concerning them which are asleep [which have died], that ye sorrow not, even as others which have no hope.

14 For if we believe that Jesus died and rose again, even so them also which sleep in Jesus will God bring with him.

15 For this we say unto you by the word of the Lord, that we which are alive and remain unto the **coming** of the Lord shall not prevent [precede] them which are asleep.

16 For the Lord himself shall descend from heaven with a shout, with the voice of the archangel, and with the trump [trumpet call] of God: and the dead in Christ shall rise first:

17 Then we which are alive and remain shall be caught up together with them in the clouds, to meet the Lord in the air: and so shall we ever be with the Lord.

18 Wherefore comfort one another with these words.

Chapter 5

1 But of the times and the seasons, brethren, ye have no need that I write unto you.

2 For yourselves know perfectly that the day of the Lord so cometh as a thief in the night.

3 For when they shall say, Peace and safety; then sudden destruction cometh upon them, as travail upon a woman with child; and they shall not escape.

---

2 Thessalonians 1:6-10; 2:1-8

Chapter 1

6 God is just: He will pay back trouble to those who trouble you

7 and give relief to you who are troubled, and to us as well. This will happen when the Lord Jesus is revealed from heaven in blazing fire with his powerful angels.

8 He will punish those who do not know God and do not obey the gospel of our Lord Jesus.

9 They will be punished with everlasting destruction and shut out from the presence of the Lord and from the majesty of his power

10 on the day he **comes** to be glorified in his holy people and to be marveled at among all those who have believed. This includes you, because you believed our testimony to you.

Chapter 2

1 Concerning the **coming** of our Lord Jesus Christ and our being gathered to him, we ask you, brothers,

2 not to become easily unsettled or alarmed by some prophecy, report or letter supposed to have come from us, saying that the day of the Lord has already come.

3 Don't let anyone deceive you in any way, for that day will not come until the rebellion occurs and the man of lawlessness is revealed, the man doomed to destruction.

4 He will oppose and will exalt himself over everything that is called God or is worshiped, so that he sets himself up in God's <u>temple</u>, proclaiming himself to be God.
5 Don't you remember that when I was with you I used to tell you these things?
6 And now you know what is holding him back, so that he may be revealed at the proper time.
7 For the secret power of lawlessness is already at work; but the one who now holds it back will continue to do so till he is taken out of the way.
8 And then the lawless one will be revealed, whom the Lord Jesus will…destroy by the splendor of his **coming**.

Revelation 1:3-7

3 Blessed is the one who reads the words of this prophecy, and blessed are those who hear it and take to heart what is written in it, because the time is near.
4 John, To the seven <u>churches</u> in the province of Asia: Grace and peace to you from him who is, and who was, and who is to come, and from the seven spirits before his throne,
5 and from Jesus Christ, who is the faithful witness, the firstborn from the dead, and the ruler of the kings of the earth. To him who loves us and has freed us from our sins by his blood,
6 and has made us to be a kingdom and priests to serve his God and Father—to him be glory and power for ever and ever! Amen.
7 <u>Look</u>, he is **coming** with the clouds, and <u>every</u> eye will see him, even those who pierced him; and all the peoples of the earth will mourn because of him. So shall it be! Amen.

Jude 1:3, 14–15 KJV

3 Beloved, when I gave all diligence to write unto you of the common salvation, it was needful for me to write unto you, and exhort *you* that ye should earnestly contend for the faith which was once delivered unto the saints.

14 And Enoch also, the seventh from Adam, prophesied of these, saying, Behold, the Lord **cometh** with ten thousands of his saints,
15 to execute judgment upon all, and to convince all that are ungodly among them of all their ungodly deeds which they have ungodly committed, and of all their hard *speeches* which ungodly sinners have spoken against him.

Section 1

Before we dig deeply into the study of the Luke 21 and Matthew 24 passages, we need to learn some things about the timing of the salvation of the remnant of Israel. (With regard to this, please also see chapter 12, section 1, part 2.)

❑ Read Daniel 9:24 *in your Bible*. Paying close attention to the timing of the salvation of Daniel's people (the Jews), would you say that Israel won't be saved (have their sins forgiven, etc.) until after the end of the seventy weeks, which equals 490 years (see the note below for an explanation of the word *week*)?

Note: The word *week* in the Hebrew language simply means seven. We think of a week as seven days, but in this prophecy, a week equals seven years. Therefore, seventy weeks is seventy multiplied by seven years.

❐ Putting together Daniel 9:24, Romans 9:27, and Romans 11:25–27 (you can look them up *in your Bible*), would you say we can safely say these things: After the 490 years, when the fullness of the Gentiles has come in, Jesus will come from Zion and take away the sins of the remnant of Israel? __________ Because Scripture says this will not take place until Jesus **comes from Zion**, we know their sins will not be taken away until Jesus is **on the earth**. ❐ True ❐ False

❐ Does Luke 21:12–17 speak of the persecution of the disciples? __________ Are those who are persecuted hated **because of Jesus** (verse 17)? __________ Does Matthew 24:9 say that those who are killed are hated by all nations for **Jesus's name's sake**? __________ Does that imply that they know and are servants of the Lord? __________

Note: Don't let the word *synagogues* in Luke 21:12 throw you. The word *synagogue* doesn't necessarily refer to a Jewish congregation; it could refer to any type of congregation according to *Strong's Exhaustive Concordance*.

❐ So now, *in your Bible*, glance again at Daniel 9:24; and in addition, read Daniel 9:27, Daniel 7:25, and Revelation 13:5–7. (With regard to the time references in the last two of those passages, read the note below.) With the knowledge of what those passages say under your belt, think about this: The abomination of desolation (aka the beast) is going to reign over the world *during* the final 3.5 years of the 490-year prophecy. However, Israel will not be saved (in other words, they won't belong to Jesus) until **after** the 490 years. Now answer this: since Israel is not saved until **after** the final 3.5 years, does it seem likely that the people of Israel, as some say, are those who will be persecuted **because of him** during those final years? __________

Note: Know that in Daniel 7:25, the final 3.5 years is referred to as a *time, times,* and *a half a time,* which is 3.5 years (a time being one year, times being two years, and a half a time being a half year). In Revelation 13:5, the 3.5 years is referred to as forty-two months.

Let's keep going.

- ❐ We saw that the ones who are killed during the reign of the abomination of desolation are persecuted **on account of the name of Jesus**. Now answer this: according to Luke 21:22–23, do we see this same period of time as a "time of punishment" (verse 22) and "wrath against this people" (verse 23)? __________ Does this seem like the same group that we read about in Luke 21:12–17 who are persecuted **on account of Jesus's name**? __________ Is being punished the same thing as being persecuted? __________

- ❐ The question that must be asked is: do those of the remnant of Israel—who will eventually be saved—actually belong to the Lord Jesus during the time of great tribulation (Matthew 24:21)? __________ In other words, are they the ones who will be persecuted for Jesus's name's sake? __________ If they are not the ones who will be persecuted during the Great Tribulation, then it must be saints who enter the time of the Great Tribulation. ❏ True ❏ False

- ❐ According to Matthew 24:3, 29–31, Jesus will return in the clouds, and the elect will be gathered by the angels at the end of the age **after** the Great Tribulation. If it is the saints who enter the tribulation period alive who are persecuted **for Jesus's name's sake**, does it seem very likely that they who are still alive are the elect who will be gathered by the angels when Jesus comes in the clouds at the end of the age? __________

Very interestingly, 1 Thessalonians 4:17 says it is those who "are alive and remain" who will be caught up in the clouds together with those who had died to meet the Lord in the air.

Let's move on.

Section 2

First, let's look for evidence that there is only one more coming of Jesus in store, in which case there will be no pre-tribulation coming of Jesus to rapture the saints.

- ☐ *Open your Bible*, and read Acts 1:6–11 and 3:20–21. Now answer this question: does it seem to you that the Lord won't leave heaven to come to earth **until** it is time to restore the kingdom to Israel? __________

- ☐ Now read Revelation 11:15 *in your Bible*, and then answer this question: does it seem to you that the kingdoms of the world will not become the kingdoms "of our Lord and of his Christ" until he comes to reign forever? __________

- ☐ Now carefully read Psalm 110:1–6 (preferably in the NASB), and then answer this question: Does it seem to you that the Lord will stay seated at the right hand of God **until** it is time to shatter kings and judge the nations? __________

- ☐ Does answering those questions affirm **there will be only one more coming** of Jesus, a coming that will not take place until it is time for Jesus to leave the right hand of God to restore the kingdom to Israel and to take over the kingdoms of the entire world, shatter kings, and judge nations? __________

Having learned that, let's look at the Matthew 24 passage.

- ❐ According to Matthew 24:30, Jesus will come on the clouds. ❏ True ❏ False

- ❐ According to Matthew 24:29–30, Jesus will come on the clouds **after** the tribulation. ❏ True ❏ False

- ❐ If there is only one coming of Jesus, then Matthew 24:30 must be speaking about his one and only second coming (he came the first time some two thousand years ago). In other words, there won't be a pre-tribulation coming of Jesus before the Matthew 24:30 post-tribulation coming of Jesus. ❏ True ❏ False

Now let's compare Matthew 24:30–31 with two other *coming* passages to see if they are speaking of the **same** coming of Jesus.

- ❐ Do both 1 Thessalonians 4:15–16 and Matthew 24:30 say Jesus will **come?** _________ Do 2 Thessalonians 1:9–10, 2:1, and 2:8 (all three verses) say Jesus will **come?** _________

- ❐ Does 1 Thessalonians 4:17 say that Jesus will come in the **clouds?** _________ Does the Matthew 24:30 say that Jesus will come on the **clouds?** _________

- ❐ According to 1 Thessalonians 4:15–17, will believers be **raptured** (caught up in the clouds) when Jesus comes? _________ According to 2 Thessalonians 2:1, will believers be **gathered** when Jesus comes? _________ Does Matthew 24:30–31 say the elect will be **gathered** when Jesus comes? _________

- ❐ Does 1 Thessalonians 4:16–17 say a **trumpet** will be heard at the coming of Jesus? _________ Does Matthew 24:30–31 say a **trumpet** will be heard at the coming of Jesus? _________

- ❐ Allowing Scripture to interpret Scripture, would you say, because of the way they tie together, Matthew 24:30, 1

Thessalonians 4:15–16, and 2 Thessalonians 1:9–10, 2:1, and 2:8 must be speaking of the same coming? ___________

☐ Now answer this: If the Scripture portions that we compared pertain to the **same** coming of Jesus, then does Matthew 24:30–31 tell us that the gathering is the rapture and that it will take place at the one and only second coming of Jesus? ___________

Second, let's find out whether or not Gentile-age believers will still be here to see the abomination of desolation standing in the holy place, claiming to be God. If they are, they will be the ones who are gathered/raptured when Jesus comes.

☐ According to Matthew 24:15, Jesus says to his disciples: "Therefore when you see the 'abomination of desolation,' spoken of by Daniel the prophet, standing in the ___________ place (whoever reads, let him understand), then let those who are in Judea flee to the mountains." (The holy place is part of God's temple.)

☐ According to 2 Thessalonians 2:1–4, Paul, the apostle to the Gentiles, says this to Gentile believers: "Concerning the coming of our Lord Jesus Christ and our being gathered to him…don't let anyone deceive you in any way, for that day will not come until…the man of lawlessness is ___________________________… [He will set] "himself up in God's ___________________, proclaiming himself to be God."

☐ Does Matthew 24:15 depict the abomination of desolation (i.e., the man of lawlessness) standing in the holy place? ___________ Does 2 Thessalonians 2:4 depict the man of lawlessness (aka the abomination of desolation) setting himself up in the temple? ___________

❑ In Matthew 24:15, does Jesus tell the disciples that they will see the abomination of desolation standing in the holy place? _____________

❑ In 2 Thessalonians 2:3–4, does Paul imply that Gentiles will be here to see the man of lawlessness setting himself up in the temple? _____________

❑ If Paul was saying that **Gentile-age believers** would see the abomination of desolation, then is it likely that Jesus also was saying that **Gentile-age believers** (a mixture of Gentile and Jewish Christians) would see the abomination of desolation? _____________

❑ Does the clear teaching 2 Thessalonians 2:1–4 say that the gathering of believers and the coming of Jesus will not occur until **after** the man of lawlessness is revealed in the temple? _____________

❑ According to the Matthew 24 passage, is it true that the coming of Jesus (verse 30) and the gathering of the elect (verse 31) do not occur until after the abomination of desolation is seen standing in the holy place (verse 15)? _____________

❑ Having learned what we have so far in this section and section 1, we can say that Gentile-age believers (those of us alive at the time) will be here to see the abomination of desolation. We can also say that we will be persecuted during the Great Tribulation, and those of us who are not killed will be gathered at the one and only second coming of Jesus, **after** the Great Tribulation. ❑ True ❑ False

Are you noticing that when Scriptures aren't explained away as meaning something other than what they truly mean, the puzzle pieces fit together beautifully?

❑ Are you taking seriously the biblical admonition to not let **anyone** deceive you in **any way**? ___________ Could there be a stronger admonition than that? __________

Third, let's look at the Revelation 1 passage and compare it to the Matthew 24 and Luke 21 *coming* passages. Why are we doing this? It is because pre-tribulationists say that those who belong to the church are not the saints of Revelation 13:5–10 who will be persecuted during the forty-two-month reign of the beast. They say that we will be raptured before that. Remember, we are comparing *coming* passages.

❑ Is Revelation 1:3–7 a coming passage? __________

❑ According to Revelation 1:5, the Book of Revelation was written to those who had been freed from their sins by the blood of Jesus. ❑ True ❑ False

❑ According to Revelation 1:4, the letter was addressed "to the seven ___________________." At the end of the Book of Revelation, we see this: "I, Jesus, have sent my angel to give you this testimony for the churches" (see Revelation 22:16 *in your Bible*). Therefore, according to those two verses, one at the beginning and one at the end of the book, and the fact that the entire Revelation letter was written to those who had been freed from their sins by the blood of Jesus, would you say the entire book is for the church? __________

❑ According to Revelation 1:3, will those who take to heart what is written in the book be blessed? __________ Does Revelation 22:16 say the testimony of the Book of Revelation is for the churches? __________ Unless someone tried to convince you otherwise, would you say the church needs to take to heart the entire book? __________

❑ The Book of Revelation was addressed to and written for the seven churches (Revelation 1:4 and 22:16), yet there is no mention of a pre-tribulation rapture. Do you find that curious? _____________

☐ Revelation 1:7 says to the churches, the congregations of those who have been freed by the blood of Jesus, "______________," he is with the clouds, and ______________ eye will see him, even those who pierced him; and all the peoples of the earth will mourn because of him." Therefore, Gentile-age (church-age) believers will look to see Jesus **at the same time** that everyone else sees him coming. ☐ True ☐ False

Read the two passages below, and then answer the question that follows the passages:

> Look, **he is coming with the clouds**, and **every eye will see him**, even those who pierced him; and all **the peoples of the earth will mourn** because of him. So shall it be! Amen. (Revelation 1:7)

> Then the sign of the Son of Man will appear in heaven and then all **the tribes of the earth will mourn**, and **they will see the Son of Man coming on the clouds** of heaven with power and great glory. And He will send His angels with a great sound of a trumpet, and they will gather together His elect from the four winds, from one end of heaven to the other. (Matthew 24:30–31)

☐ What details link the two passages above together?

❑ Pay really close attention now. Because of the ways the two passages above link together, would you say that Matthew 24:30–31, like Revelation 1:7, is saying that it is the church (i.e., the saints) who will see Jesus coming in the clouds? __________ And would you say that it is the church who will be gathered (raptured) when he comes (verse 31)? __________

Another passage to consider regarding this issue is Luke 21:27–28. That will be addressed in section 3.

Some pre-tribulationists say the saints of Revelation 13:5–10 who will be persecuted by the beast cannot be members of the church but rather are people that are saved after the rapture. They defend this by saying the word *church* is not mentioned again in the book after the third chapter. They say it even though the plural form of it is (see Revelation 22:16 *in your Bible*). Regarding that, answer these questions:

❑ Is the church made up of saints? __________

❑ In the Book of Jude, which was written to the saints to encourage them to contend for the faith (1:3), the word church is not mentioned. The letter was written to the saints, but because the word church is not mentioned in the book, what is in it does not pertain to the church but, rather, some other group. ❑ True ❑ False

❑ The word church is absent in many chapters in the books of the New Testament. That means that those chapters do not pertain to the church. ❑ True ❑ False

Note: I hope you checked the false box for the last two questions.

❑ Knowing what you know so far, would you say that the saints of Revelation 13:7–10 (look it up *in your Bible*) are indeed members of the church? __________ Will the church be persecuted? __________

If there will be no pre-tribulation rapture, the entire Book of Revelation is for Gentile-age believing saints. That means we need to "take to heart what is written in it" and remember that we will be blessed by hearing it (Revelation 1:3). Here is just some of what we should take to heart:

> Then I heard a voice from heaven say, "Write: Blessed are the dead who die in the Lord from now on." "Yes," says the Spirit, "they will rest from their labor, for their deeds will follow them." (Revelation 14:13)

> Then one of the elders asked me, "These in white robes—who are they, and where did they come from?" I answered, "Sir, you know." And he said, "These are they who have come out of the great tribulation; they have washed their robes and made them white in the blood of the Lamb. Therefore, they are before the throne of God and serve him day and night in his temple; and he who sits on the throne will spread his tent over them. Never again will they hunger; never again will they thirst. The sun will not beat upon them, nor any scorching heat. For the Lamb at the center of the throne will be their shepherd; he will lead them to springs of living water. And God will wipe away every tear from their eyes." (Revelation 7:13–17)

Fourth, let's link three of the passages to find out if—at the same coming of Jesus—unbelievers and the man of lawlessness are destroyed, and the saints are raptured/gathered:

❐ Read the 1 Thessalonians passage. Now answer this question: Will sudden destruction come upon unbelievers when Jesus comes (verse 4:16 and 5:3)? _________ Will those who are alive and remain be caught up (raptured) to meet Jesus when he comes (verse 4:17)? ___________

❑ Does the 2 Thessalonians passage teach that unbelievers will be punished with everlasting destruction when Jesus comes (1:9-10)? ___________ Will the man of lawlessness be destroyed when Jesus comes (2:8)? ___________ Will we be raptured when he comes (2:1)? ___________

❑ Does Jude 1:14–15 say Jesus will execute judgment upon all the ungodly sinners when he comes? ___________

❑ Does Jude 1:14 say Jesus will come with his saints? ___________

❑ Does 1 Thessalonians 4:14 teach that Jesus will come with the saints? ___________

❑ Because of the linking of the three coming passages, do you agree that these four things will occur at the **same** coming of Jesus: (1) saints will return with Jesus, (2) sinners will be punished with destruction, (3) the man of lawlessness will be destroyed, and (4) those of us who are still alive will be raptured (caught up) to meet Jesus? ___________

❑ If the destruction of sinners and the man of lawlessness take place at the coming of Jesus and we are raptured at that time, do you agree that the rapture will not take place until the end of the age, an age that will not end until after the Great Tribulation (Matthew 24:3, 29–31)? ___________

Section 3

Pay very close attention to what is coming up here. We are going to find out who will be redeemed when Jesus comes.

Please read the passage below (Luke 21:25–28), which I copied from the main Luke 21 passage.

> **25** And there will be signs in the sun, in the moon, and in the stars; and on the earth distress of nations, with perplexity, the sea and the waves roaring;
> **26** men's hearts failing them from fear and the expectation of those things which are coming on the earth, for the powers of the heavens will be shaken.
> **27** Then they will see the Son of Man coming in a cloud with power and great glory.
> **28** Now when these things begin to happen, look up and lift up your heads, because your redemption draws near.

In the passage above, underline the things that will take place before the coming of Jesus and the redemption of believers that verse 28 mentions.

- ❏ According to verse 28, is it when those things (the things you underlined) begin to happen that those who are about to be redeemed are to look up and lift up their heads?
  ❏ True ❏ False

- ❏ According to verses 27-28, when they lift up their heads, who will they see? ___________________

Let's find out who will be redeemed when Jesus comes.

- ❏ Paul, the apostle to the Gentiles, wrote to Gentile believers and said this: "And do not grieve the Holy Spirit of God, with whom you were sealed for the day of redemption" (Ephesians 4:30). Did you catch the fact that the Gentiles were sealed for the day of redemption? __________

❑ Therefore, it is Gentile-age believers (which, of course, includes some Jewish believers) who are sealed for the day of redemption and are told to lift up their heads to see Jesus coming in a cloud (verses 27–28). ❑ True ❑ False

❑ Recalling the things you underlined, things that will take place before our redemption, would you say our redemption will take place at the end of the age? ___________

Compare Luke 21:25–28 (quoted just a little ways above) with Matthew 24:29–31 below (copied from the main Matthew 24 passage):

> **29** Immediately after the tribulation of those days the sun will be darkened, and the moon will not give its light; the stars will fall from heaven, and the powers of the heavens will be shaken.
> **30** Then the sign of the Son of Man will appear in heaven and then all the tribes of the earth will mourn, and they will see the Son of Man coming on the clouds of heaven with power and great glory.
> **31** And He will send His angels with a great sound of a trumpet, and they will gather together His elect from the four winds, from one end of heaven to the other.

❑ Do you agree that both passages speak of the same event? ___________

❑ We learned from the Luke 21 passage and Ephesians 4:30, it is **Gentile-age believers** who are about to be redeemed when Jesus is seen coming; therefore, in the Matthew 24 passage, it is **Gentile-age believers** who are about to be gathered when Jesus is seen coming. ❑ True ❑ False

❑ We see in the Matthew 24 passage that this gathering will take place after the tribulation of those days (verse 29). ❑ True ❑ False

Note: According to *The Apostolic Bible Polyglot* (a Greek Old and New Testament numerically coded Bible), the word *redemption* is mentioned quite a bit in the Old Testament, but it is *not* the same word as the word *redemption* in the New Testament. And the word *redemption* found in the New Testament is not mentioned at all in the Old Testament.

Taking into consideration all that you learned from this chapter, answer the following questions:

❑ Do you believe there is only one coming of Jesus yet to come? _____________

❑ Do you believe that Jesus's coming will not take place until it is time for Jesus to leave the right hand of God to take over the kingdom of the world and shatter kings and judge nations? _____________

❑ Do you believe that it will be Gentiles-age believers (consisting of mostly Gentile but some Jewish believers also) who will lift up their heads and be raptured (gathered) and redeemed when Jesus comes after the time of tribulation? _____________

Record here anything that you disagree with or are not sure about:

____

____

____

____

____

Are you in awe yet of the many ways God tries to reach us with the truth? I could have written even more chapters proving that the rapture will not occur until after the tribulation, but what has been written seems sufficient.

This is a good time for these words of admonition and encouragement: "Therefore, prepare your minds for action; be self-controlled; set your hope fully on the grace to be given you when Jesus Christ is revealed" (1 Peter 1:13–14).

Chapter 11
Preparation for Tribulation

Those who are born again by the Spirit of God know they have eternal life. God downloads that glorious truth into their hearts. If God has not made known to you that you have eternal life, read chapter 13, "The Glorious Gospel of Jesus Christ," and believe what you read, for we are saved by faith.

The passages in this chapter will help prepare you for persecution. Read each passage in its entirety. As you go along, notice that almost every passage that speaks of the persecution for which believers are destined also speaks of the blessings that will be received by those who endure.

In this chapter, you are asked to read most of the passages *in your Bible* because, according to the publisher, there was a limit to the number of passages I could quote in the book.

Luke 6:21–23

21 [Jesus said,] "Blessed are you who hunger now, for you will be satisfied. Blessed are you who weep now, for you will laugh.
22 "Blessed are you when men hate you, when they exclude you and insult you and reject your name as evil, because of the Son of Man.

23 "Rejoice in that day and leap for joy, because great is your reward in heaven. For that is how their fathers treated the prophets."

Read the passage above, and then answer these questions:

❑ Finish the two sentences that begin with "Blessed are you" in verse 21:

❑ According to verse 22, blessed are you when:

❑ According to verse 23, what are these blessed ones to do, and why are they to do it?

---

2 Timothy 1:7–8

Read 2 Timothy 1:7–8 in your Bible, and then answer these questions:

❑ According to verse 8, believers should not be ashamed of what?

❏ According to that same verse, what did Paul want Timothy to join with him in doing?

Philippians 1:27–30

Read Philippians 1:27–30 in your Bible, and then answer these questions:

❏ According to verse 28, should believers be frightened by those who oppose them? __________

❏ According to verse 29, what two things were granted to the Philippian believers?

Philippians 4:12–13

Read Philippians 4:12–13 in your Bible, and then answer these questions:

❏ According to verse 12, what did Paul, the writer of the letter, learn the secret of?

❏ According to verse 13, could Paul do those things in his own strength? __________

Revelation 17:12-14

Read Revelation 17:12–14 in your Bible, and then answer these questions:

☐ According to verses 12–14, when the ten kings and the beast go to war against the Lamb, what will the outcome be?

☐ According to verse 14, who will be with Jesus when he overcomes the beast and the ten kings?

---

1 Thessalonians 3:2-13

2 We sent Timothy, who is our brother and God's fellow worker in spreading the gospel of Christ, to strengthen and encourage you in your <u>faith</u>,
3 so that no one would be <u>unsettled</u> by these trials. You know quite well that we were <u>destined</u> for them.
4 In fact, when we were with you, we kept telling you that we would be <u>persecuted</u>. And it turned out that way, as you well know.
5 For this reason, when I could stand it no longer, I sent to find out about your faith. I was afraid that in some way the tempter might have tempted you and our efforts might have been useless.
6 But Timothy has just now come to us from you and has brought good news about your <u>faith</u> and <u>love</u>. He has told us that you always have pleasant

memories of us and that you long to see us, just as we also long to see you.

7 Therefore, brothers, in all our distress and persecution we were encouraged about you because of your faith.

8 For now we really live, since you are standing firm in the Lord.

9 How can we thank God enough for you in return for all the joy we have in the presence of our God because of you?

10 Night and day we pray most <u>earnestly</u> that we may see you again and supply what is lacking in your <u>faith</u>.

11 Now may our God and Father himself and our Lord Jesus clear the way for us to come to you.

12 May the Lord make your love increase and overflow for each other and for everyone else, just as ours does for you.

13 May he strengthen your hearts so that you will be blameless and <u>holy</u> in the presence of our <u>God</u> and Father <u>when</u> our Lord Jesus <u>comes</u> with all his holy ones [saints].

Read the passage above, and then answer these questions:

☐ Verses 2–3 say, "We sent Timothy, who is our brother and God's fellow worker in spreading the gospel of Christ, to strengthen and encourage you in your _________________, so that no one would be _____________________ by these. You know quite well that we were _____________________ for them."

☐ If we are not prepared for trials, could they unsettle us? _________

❏ According to verse 4, the writers kept telling the Thessalonians that they "would be ___________."

❏ According to that same verse, were they persecuted? ___________

❏ According to verse 6, Timothy brought back to Paul good news about their ___________ and ___________.

❏ According to verse 10, Paul, Silas, and Timothy prayed night and day most ___________ that they would be able to see them again to supply what was lacking in their ___________.

❏ According to verse 12, what did Paul, Silas, and Timothy pray?

❏ According to verse 13, the writers prayed, "May he strengthen your hearts so that you will be blameless and ___________ in the presence of our ___________ and Father ___________ our Lord Jesus ___________ with all his holy ones [saints]."

❏ Do your elders, as far as you are aware, have the same concern for their sheep as Paul, Silas, and Timothy had for the Thessalonians? ___________ Do they pray for you the way Paul, Silas, and Timothy did for the Thessalonians? ___________ Do you pray for your fellow saints as they did? ___________

Hebrews 10:32–39

32 Remember those earlier days after you had received the light, when you stood your ground in a great contest in the face of suffering.
33 Sometimes you were publicly exposed to <u>insult</u> and <u>persecution</u>; at other times you stood side by side with those who were so <u>treated</u>.

34 You sympathized with those in <u>prison</u> and <u>joyfully</u> accepted the confiscation of your property, because you knew that you yourselves had better and lasting possessions.

35 So do not throw away your confidence; it will be richly rewarded.

36 You need to persevere so that when you have done the will of God, you will receive what he has promised.

37 For in just a very little while, "He who is coming will come and will not delay."

38 But my righteous one will live by faith. And if he shrinks back, I will not be pleased with him.

39 But we are not of those who shrink back and are destroyed, but of those who believe and are saved.

Read the passage above, and then answer these questions:

- ❐ According to verse 33, sometimes they were "exposed to ____________________ and ______________________________ ______________; at other times they "stood side by side with those who were so ___________________."

- ❐ According to verse 34, they "sympathized with those in ____________________ and ______________________ accepted the confiscation" of their property.

- ❐ According to that same verse, why did they joyfully accept the confiscation of their property?

- ❐ According to verse 36, what do believers need to do to receive what God has promised us?

❑ According to verse 37, what were they told would happen in a very little while?

❑ According to verse 38, do the righteous live by the works they have done or by faith?

❑ According to verse 39, what did the writer of the Book of Hebrews say to these believers?

---

1 Peter 1:3-9

3 Praise be to the God and Father of our Lord Jesus Christ! In his great mercy he has given us new birth into a living hope through the resurrection of Jesus Christ from the dead,
4 and into an inheritance that can never perish, spoil or fade—kept in heaven for you,
5 who through <u>faith</u> are shielded by God's power until the coming of the salvation that is ready to be revealed in the last time.
6 In this you greatly rejoice, though now for a <u>little</u> while you may have had to suffer <u>grief</u> in all kinds of <u>trials</u>.
7 These have come so that your faith—of greater worth than <u>gold</u>, which perishes even though refined by fire—may be proved genuine and may result in praise, glory and honor when Jesus Christ is revealed.

> **8** Though you have not seen him, you love him; and even though you do not see him now, you believe in him and are filled with an inexpressible and glorious joy,
> **9** for you are receiving the goal of your faith, the salvation of your souls.

Read the passage above, and then answer these questions:

- ❏ Verse 5 tells us that "through _______________ [believers] are shielded by God's power until the coming of the salvation that is ready to be revealed in the last time."

- ❏ Verse 6 says the believers greatly rejoiced, even though for a _______________ while they had to suffer _______________ in all kinds of _______________.

- ❏ Verse 7 says a believer's faith (the kind of faith that sustains us through trials and persecution) is "of greater worth than _______________."

- ❏ According to that same verse, what will it result in and when?

---

1 Peter 2:19–25

Read 1 Peter 2:19–25 in your Bible, and then answer these questions:

- ❏ According to verse 20, what is commendable before God?

❏ According to verse 23, did Jesus retaliate when insults were hurled at him? ___________ Did he make threats when he suffered? ___________ What did he do instead?

---

1 Peter 4:12-14

Read 1 Peter 4:12–14 in your Bible, and then answer these questions:

❏ According to verse 12, should we be surprised when we face fiery ordeals? ___________

❏ According to verse 13, why should we rejoice when we participate in the sufferings of Christ?

❏ According to verse 14, if we are insulted for the name of Christ, are we blessed? ___________ Why are we blessed?

Acts 20:22-24; Acts 8:1, 4; John 4:4-42

Read Acts 20:22–24 in your Bible, and then answer these questions:

❏ According to verse 23, what did the Holy Spirit warn Paul about?

❐ According to verse 24, who gave him a task to complete, and what was that task?

Read Acts 8:1 and 4 in your Bible, and then answer this question:

❐ According to those two verses, when persecution broke out, and there was a scattering, was it the apostles or just ordinary believers who preached the gospel in Judea and Samaria?

Read John 4:4–42 in your Bible, and then answer these questions:

❐ According to verses 28–29, what did the Samaritan woman do and say when she went into the city?

❐ According to verses 39–42, what was the final result?

John 21:18-19

Read John 21:18–19 in your Bible, and then answer these questions:

❐ According to verse 18, Jesus told Peter that he would be led to where he did not want to go. ❐ True ❐ False

❏ According to verse 19, does the death of a believer by the hands of unbelievers glorify God? _________

Mark 13:1–37

Read Mark 13:1–37 in your Bible, and then answer these questions:

❏ According to verse 5, Jesus tells believers to "watch out that no one deceives" them. Why, according to verse 6, must believers watch out?

❏ According to verses 9, 12, and 13, what will happen to believers?

❏ According to verse 13, we will be hated because of who?
____

❏ According to verse 11, are we to worry about what to say when brought to trial? _________ Why?

❏ According to verse 20, for whose sake will the days be shortened?

❏ According to verse 21–22, who and what are we not to believe?

❏ Matthew 24:30 says all the nations will see Jesus when he comes in the clouds. Likewise, Revelation 1:7 says every eye will see him when he comes in the clouds. Therefore, if someone says he's out in the desert or in an inner room and you haven't seen him come in the clouds, should you believe it? ___________

❐ According to verse 23, has Jesus told us everything we need to know? ___________ If he told us things we need to know, should we listen to him? ___________

❐ According to verse 33, when the time comes, why should we be on guard and alert?

❐ According to verse 34, each of us has an assigned ______________.

❐ Quote verse 35 in its entirety below, paying very close attention to the very short period of time wherein we will not know when the owner of the house will come back.

❐ According to verse 37, should just some or all watch?
❑ Just some ❑ All

❐ What are the signs in verses 24–26 that will precede the coming of Jesus in the clouds?

❐ Because of the signs mentioned in those verses, we will know the approximate time of his return. ❑ True ❑ False

❐ Answer this question, giving it serious consideration: Do you think that some of those who believe they will not be here during the Great Tribulation (because they believe they will be raptured out of here before then) will pay much attention to everything Jesus said in Mark 13, Matthew 24–25, Luke 17:20–37 and 21:5–36, or Daniel or Revelation, etc., to try to prepare us for that time? ___________

Hebrews 11:35-40

Read Hebrews 11:35–40 in your Bible, and then answer these questions:

- ☐ What are some of the ways the Old Testament saints were persecuted?

- ☐ According to verse 39, were they commended for their faith?
  ____

- ☐ According to verses 39–40, did they receive what had been promised at that time? ___________

- ☐ According to verse 40, will the Old Testament believers be made perfect at the same time as the New Testament believers?
  ____

Romans 8:35-39

Read Romans 8:35–39, and then answer this question:

- ☐ Will trouble, hardship, persecution, famine, nakedness, danger, sword, death, life, angels, demons, or anything else in all creation be able to separate us from the love of God? ___________

Revelation 2:7B, 11B, 17B, 26-28; 3:5, 12, 21

As you read the following verses, preferably in the KJV or the NASB because the word used in each of the verses to translate G3528 is *overcomes*, record under each reference what is in store for those who overcome.

❏ 2:7b

❏ 2:11b

❏ 2:17b

❏ 2:26–28

❏ 3:5

❏ 3:12

❏ 3:21

We just learned all the wonderful things that are in store for those who overcome. Learn and absorb from this passage who it is that overcomes:

> Everyone who believes that Jesus is the Christ is born of God, and everyone who loves the father loves his child as well. This is how we know that we love the children of God: by loving God and carrying out his commands. This is love for God: to obey his commands. And his commands are not burdensome, for everyone born of God over- comes the world. This is the victory that has **overcome** the world, **even our faith**. Who is it that **overcomes** the world? **Only he who believes that Jesus is the Son of God**. (1 John 5:1–5)

---

1 Thessalonians 4:13-18

Read 1 Thessalonians 4:13–18 in your Bible, then answer these questions:

- ❑ According to the passage, did Paul inform the believers that not only would they always be with the Lord after his return but also those who had died (fallen asleep)? __________ Did Paul tell the believers to be comforted (encouraged) by that fact (verse 18)? __________

- ❑ Therefore, Paul wasn't saying (as some of the pre-tribula- tionists say) that they would be raptured before the Great Tribulation and should be comforted because they would escape persecution. Rather, according to the context of the passage, he was saying that they should be comforted by the fact that they would be reunited with those who had died and that they then together would always be with the Lord. ❑ True ❑ False

Acts 5:40-42

Read Acts 5:40–42 in your Bible, and then answer these questions:

- ☐ According to verse 40, what were the apostles ordered to do by the false religious leaders?

- ☐ According to verses 41, what was the reaction of the apostles who had just been flogged for speaking about Jesus?

- ☐ According to verse 42, what did the apostles continue to do?

Philippians 1:12-14

Read Philippians 1:12–14, then answer this question:

- ☐ According to verse 12–14, what was the result of Paul's chains/ imprisonment?

2 Corinthians 5:8-9

8 We are confident, I say, and would prefer to be away from the body and at <u>home</u> with the <u>Lord</u>.
9 So we make it our goal to please him, whether we are at home in the body or away from it.

Read the passage above, and then answer these questions:

❒ When a believer is "away from the body," he is "at ______________ with the ______________."

❒ Are you afraid to die? __________

Matthew 25:1-13

Read Matthew 25:1–13 in your Bible, and then answer these questions:

❒ In verse 12, what did Jesus say to the virgins who were not ready?

❒ Are you confident that Jesus will not say that to you? __________

❒ Do you have a relationship with him (i.e., does he know you?) __________ (If you answered "no" or are not absolutely sure, read chapter 13 to find out how you can begin a relationship with him.)

Matthew 10:28

28 Do not be afraid of those who kill the body but cannot kill the soul. Rather, be afraid of the <u>One</u> who can destroy both soul and body in hell.

Read the verse above, and then give your answers:

☐ According to that verse, should we be afraid of those who have the power to kill us? __________ Rather, we should fear "the ______ who can destroy both soul and body in hell."

Chapter 12

Responses to Some of the Pre-Tribulation Arguments

My understanding of the timing of the rapture didn't come easily. It took a great deal of study of the pure milk of God's holy Word that he so graciously and lovingly gave to us. Many links needed to be made. Blinders from false teaching needed to be removed. Countless questions needed to be answered. A lot of confusion needed to be cleared up. I still have a lot of questions and always will, but because many of the questions have been answered, the remaining questions will be more easily answered. The more pieces of the puzzle that are in their proper places, the easier it becomes to fit the remaining pieces in their places.

I thank Jesus that he has given me, a very ordinary person, the understanding I have. If he did that for me, he will do that for anyone willing to sit at his feet to learn from him.

If at any time the Lord shows me Scripture that conflicts with my understanding, I will alter what I believe. We should always to ready to correct our beliefs if shown by Scripture that we are wrong. We should never elevate our word over the Word of God.

Section 1: Will Jews Be the Ones to Undergo Persecution During the Great Tribulation?

This was mentioned before, but I will mention it again: because pre-tribulationists say that the rapture will take place before the Great Tribulation, they must explain away Matthew 24:31 as being something other than the rapture because Matthew 24:29–31 clearly states that the gathering will be preceded by the "tribulation of those days," referred to in Matthew 24:21 as "great tribulation." Some say that the gathering in that verse is the gathering of Jews to the land of Israel upon Christ's return, and that it will be Jews who will be persecuted by the beast during his reign. I agree that Jews **will** be gathered to the land upon the return of Jesus, but is that what Matthew 24:31 portrays? And is it the Jews who will be persecuted during the Great Tribulation? (Please also read chapter 10 if you haven't already.) Parts 1–4 below will reveal why I think that it will be believers—not Jews—who will be persecuted during the Great Tribulation.

Part 1: The End-Time Scenario

There is a lot more to the story than what follows, but my summary of end-times will help explain the big picture of what I believe. To make what follows easier to read, I have not cluttered it up with a lot of references (just some). However, many of the Scriptures that my understanding come from are quoted throughout the book.

> At a certain point in time, Satan will be thrown down to earth, never to be allowed back in heaven again. He will then know that his time is short and, because of that, will be filled with great fury (Revelation 12:7–8, 12).

> When the beast (also known as the abomination of desolation and the man of lawlessness) comes out of the abyss, Satan will transfer to him his

power, throne, and authority. The beast will then reign over all the nations and will make war with the saints for a period of forty-two months (3.5 years).

At the beginning of this 3.5-year period of great tribulation, the abomination of desolation will stand in the holy place (the temple yet to be built) in Jerusalem, claiming to be God. Armies will surround Jerusalem, and the city will be trampled on by Gentiles until Jesus returns, for it will be "the time of punishment in fulfillment of all that has been written [in the Old Testament]" (Luke 21:22). "There will be great distress in the land and wrath against this people [the people of Israel]" (Luke 21:23).

During this predicted time of punishment of the nation of Israel, they "will fall by the edge of the sword and taken as prisoners to all the nations" (Luke 21:24). Not all will die; a remnant of Jews will be protected from the beast's onslaught.

Saints will know it is time to flee Judea when they see armies surrounding Jerusalem and the abomination of desolation standing where it does not belong. Among other things, Jesus says to them: "You will be hated by all because of My name, but it is the one who has endured to the end who will be saved. When you are persecuted in one place, flee to another. I tell you the truth, you will not finish going through the cities of Israel before the Son of Man comes" (Matthew 10:22–23).

During the time of the beast's rule—the worst times the world has ever seen—he will persecute believers throughout the world precisely because they will refuse to worship him and receive his mark. Because the days will be cut short, there will be survivors. Those survivors are the elect of Matthew 24:31. They will be gathered by the angels and caught up to meet Jesus in the air when he comes.

Just as Lot was pulled out of Sodom immediately before it was destroyed, believers in Jesus who survive the Great Tribulation will be caught up to meet Jesus just before, in his great wrath, he destroys all the unrepentant sinners of the world. These precious believers will not suffer the wrath of the Lamb but will instead receive salvation (1 Thessalonians 5:9).

Upon the Lord's return, the remnant of Jews whose lives the Lord will protect during the time of punishment of Israel, after calling on his name, will be forgiven, given new hearts, and grafted back into the olive tree (see Romans 11:24–27). The end of the 490-day prophecy in Daniel 9 regarding Israel will have come, and they will sin no more. Jesus will settle these humble and repentant Jews in their land. God will be their God and will cause them to flourish and have children. They will never fear again.

Some Gentiles will also survive the Great Tribulation and will believe when Jesus returns. They, along with the Jews, will populate the earth during the thousand-year reign of our Lord and King, Jesus Christ, the Son of God.

> Those who had believed before the coming of
> Jesus will have glorified bodies (like our Lord's
> body after he rose from the dead), will sin no
> more, and will reign with Christ in Jerusalem.
> They will be like the angels in that they will not
> marry or have children.

Part 2: When Will God Save the Remnant of Jews?

Luke 21:12–24 talks about the persecution of some and the punishment of others. Being persecuted and being punished are very different things. Jew and Gentile believers will be persecuted because of their faith in Jesus; unbelieving Jews will be punished, as was prophesied in the Old Testament (Luke 21:22), because of their sins, unrepentant hearts, and hostility toward God. The Old Testament is full of passages that speak of the punishment of Israel. Here is one: "The days of punishment are coming, the days of reckoning are at hand. Let Israel know this. Because your sins are so many and your hostility so great, the prophet is considered a fool, the inspired man a maniac" (Hosea 9:7). However, a remnant of Jews will survive and Old Testament prophecies regarding Israel will come true!

A reading of the passages below reveals that the Jewish remnant that had been rejected by the Lord will not be saved **until** Jesus comes back to the earth at the end of the current age. That means they cannot be the believers who are persecuted during the time of the Great Tribulation, for those who go through that time of tribulation are persecuted **on account of the name of Jesus** (Luke 21:12), their Lord.

> Then the Lord will appear over them; his arrow
> will flash like lightning. The Sovereign Lord will
> sound the trumpet; he will march in the storms
> of the south, and the Lord Almighty will shield
> them. They will destroy and overcome with

slingstones. They will drink and roar as with wine; they will be full like a bowl used for sprinkling the corners of the altar. The Lord their God will save them on that day [that he appears over them] as a flock of his people. They will sparkle in his land like jewels in a crown. How attractive and beautiful they will be! Grain will make the young men thrive, and new wine the young women. (Zechariah 9:14–17)

I do not want you to be ignorant of this mystery, brothers, so that you may not be conceited: Israel has experienced a hardening in part until the full number of the Gentiles has come in. And so all Israel will be saved, as it is written: **"The deliverer will come from Zion; he will turn godlessness away from Jacob**. And this is my covenant with them when I take away their sins." (Romans 11:25–27)

"I am going to bring my servant, the Branch… and **I will remove the sin of this land in a single day**. In that day each of you will invite his neighbor to sit under his vine and fig tree," declares the Lord Almighty. (Zechariah 3:8–10)

[The Lord said], "I will show wonders in the heavens and on the earth, blood and fire and billows of smoke. The sun will be turned to darkness and the moon to blood before the coming of the great and dreadful day of the Lord. And everyone who calls on the name of the Lord will be saved; for on Mount Zion and in Jerusalem there will be deliverance, as the Lord has said, among the survivors whom the Lord calls." (Joel 2:30–32)

> [The Lord declares,] "And I will pour out on the house of David and the inhabitants of Jerusalem a spirit of grace and supplication. They will look on me, the one they have pierced, and they will mourn for him as one mourns for an only child, and grieve bitterly for him as one grieves for a firstborn son. On that day the weeping in Jerusalem will be as great as the weeping of Hadad Rimmon in the plain of Megiddo. The land will mourn, each clan by itself, with their wives by themselves: the clan of the house of David and their wives, the clan of the house of Nathan and their wives, the clan of the house of Levi and their wives, the clan of Shimei and their wives, and all the rest of the clans and their wives. On that day a fountain will be opened to the house of David and the inhabitants of Jerusalem, to cleanse them from sin and impurity." (Zechariah 12:10–13:1)

Part 3: Who Are the Elect?

The word *elect* is used three times in Matthew 24 (see verses 22, 24, and 31). The elect mentioned in Matthew 24:31 are the ones who will be gathered by the angels. Who are these elect? Let's find out.

Paul, a Jew, was an apostle appointed to preach the gospel to the Gentiles (Galatians 2:7). The passage below is very informative. To me it reveals that it is only the saved ones of Israel that are referred to as the elect. As was said in the last section, the remnant of Israel will not be saved until after the time of tribulation. That means they cannot be the elect of Matthew 24 because the elect in Matthew 24 are believers in Jesus.

> So too, at the present time, there is a remnant chosen by grace. And if by grace, then it cannot

be based on works; if it were, grace would no longer be grace. What then? **What the people of Israel sought so earnestly they did not obtain. The elect among them did**, but the others were hardened. (Romans 11:5–7)

This word *elect*, according to *The Apostolic Bible Polyglot*, is not even in the Old Testament. Israel is a chosen nation, but that word *chosen* used to describe Israel in the Old Testament is not the same word as the word *elect* in the New Testament. I think this passage tells us what Israel was chosen for. It is not the same thing as being chosen for salvation:

> For I could wish that I myself were accursed, separated from Christ for the sake of my countrymen, my kinsmen according to the flesh, who are Israelites, to whom belongs the adoption as sons and daughters, the glory, the covenants, the giving of the Law, the temple service, and the promises; whose are the fathers, and from whom is the Christ according to the flesh, who is over all, God blessed forever. Amen. (Romans 9:3–5, NASB)

Part 4: Who Are They That Come Out of the Great Tribulation?

In the Book of Revelation, we read that those who will come out of the Great Tribulation will be a great multitude from every tribe, language, nation, and people, making it clear that those who will go through the Great Tribulation will not be a remnant of Jews!

> After this I looked, and there before me was **a great multitude that no one could count, from every nation, tribe, people and language, standing before the throne and in front of the**

Lamb. They were wearing white robes and were holding palm branches in their hands… Then one of the elders asked me, "These in white robes—who are they, and where did they come from?" I answered, "Sir, you know." And he said, **"These are they who have come out of the great tribulation; they have washed their robes and made them white in the blood of the Lamb."** (Revelation 7:9, 13–14)

Section 2: Will It Be Newly Saved Saints or Mature Saints Who Are Persecuted?

Saints will be persecuted during the reign of the beast. Some say that those persecuted will be individuals who are saved **after** a supposed pre-tribulation rapture, not the saints who are alive at the time and enter the time of great tribulation. Before we do anything else, let's simply look at passages that tell us about the persecution of the saints.

The beast was given a mouth to utter proud words and blasphemies and to exercise his authority for forty-two months [3.5 years]. He opened his mouth to blaspheme God and to slander his name and his dwelling place and those who live in heaven. He was given power to make war against the saints and to conquer them. And he was given authority over every tribe, people, language, and nation. All inhabitants of the earth will worship the beast—all whose names have not been written in the book of life belonging to the Lamb that was slain from the creation of the world. He who has an ear, let him hear. If anyone is to go into captivity, into captivity he will go. If anyone is to be killed with the sword, with the sword he will be killed. This calls for

> patient endurance and faithfulness on the part of
> the saints. (Revelation 13:5–10)

> You will be betrayed even by parents, brothers,
> relatives and friends, and they will put some of
> you to death. All men will hate you because of
> me [Jesus]. (Luke 21:16–17)

Okay, so now you know what it will be like for the saints who are going to be persecuted. The pre-tribulationists tell us that God would not allow persecution of his saints, yet we know that some saints **will** be persecuted. Here is a question I ask myself: if God would not allow persecution of the more mature saints, why on earth would he allow persecution of the "baby" saints?

Section 3: Are the 144,000 Jewish Evangelists?

Many pre-tribulationists say that the 144,000 are Jewish evangelists who preach the gospel after a supposed pre-tribulation rapture. They say that it is through the preaching of the gospel by these evangelists that people will be saved.

I cannot say for sure who I think the 144,000 are, but this I know: nowhere in the Book of Revelation does it say they are evangelists. They are mentioned in three places in the Book of Revelation. You can go to the passages to see for yourself: Revelation 7:1–8, 9:4, and 14:1–5.

Section 4: Will Anyone Be Saved During the Great Tribulation?

I am not absolutely certain about this because I haven't studied this point enough, but I don't think anyone will be saved during the Great

Tribulation. Before it, yes. After it, yes. During it, no. I have not yet come across any verse or passage that says people will be saved during the reign of the beast. In the Book of Revelation, we see that they hear the gospel (Revelation 14:6–7) but refuse to repent (Revelation 9:20 and Revelation 16:10–11). If it is the case the no one will be saved during the time of tribulation, that would be evidence that those saved before the Great Tribulation will be the ones who will be persecuted during it. Here are some other passages that make me lean toward believing that no one will be saved during that time: 2 Thessalonians 2:9–12, Revelation 22:11, and Daniel 12:5–10.

If my understanding is correct, now is the time to preach the gospel to your loved ones (and others as well)!

Section 5: Will the Raptured Saints Return to Earth With Jesus?

In defense of their position, some pre-tribulationists say that it cannot be a post-tribulation rapture because it would be ridiculous for the Lord to gather believers up to the clouds to meet him in the air and then bring them back down to earth. But I ask this question: why do they not say that it would be ridiculous for the Lord to bring those who had fallen asleep down from heaven only to take them back to heaven?

I don't think raptured believers will go to heaven after the rapture. It seems to me they will meet Jesus in the clouds and then come back with him. "When Christ, who is your life, appears, then you also will appear with him in glory" (Colossians 3:4). First Thessalonians 4:17 says we will be with Jesus forever after the rapture; so unless he goes back to heaven, which he will not, we will not go to heaven. Revelation 17:12–14 says we will be with the Lamb when the ten kings and the beast make war against him. Scripture teaches that when he comes, he will begin to rule and reign on the earth and that we will reign with him (Daniel 7:27, Revelation 5:10).

Could one of the purposes of meeting Jesus in the clouds be to greet our King and welcome him to the earth? To find the answer to that, we need to explore the meaning of the word *meet* in 1 Thessalonians 4:17. Start at this website, and then do more exploring on your own if you wish: https://openoureyeslord.com/2011/05/25/1-thess-417-meet-the-lord-in-the-air-in-the-original-greek/. (Disclaimer: I found this website in search of the meaning of the word *meet* in 1 Thessalonians 4:17. While it may contain good and accurate teaching, I have not read enough of the teaching on the website to vouch for all of it.)

Section 6: Who/What Is the Restraining Force?

Second Thessalonians 2:3–8 says the lawless one will not be revealed until "he" is removed (verse 7). The pre-tributationists (at least some of them) teach that "he" is the Holy Spirit and that he must be removed before the man of lawlessness can be revealed. If I understand their take, they don't believe the Holy Spirit will be removed entirely, just the power of his work in believers.

In my opinion, there is a serious problem with this teaching: the Second Letter to Thessalonians 2:6–7 does not say that the work of the Holy Spirit in believers will be removed, and it doesn't even say that the "he" **is** the Holy Spirit. That begs the question, why would they teach that? Well, they really don't even try to hide the fact that they teach that to support their pre-tribulation rapture position. For they say the removal of the Holy Spirit means the church will be removed. That, then, would make the rapture a pre-tribulation event, for the Great Tribulation will not commence until after the man of lawlessness is revealed.

If the Holy Spirit isn't "he" of 2:7, then who is? And what is the "what" of 2:6? If one doesn't try to use 2 Thessalonians 2:6 and 7 to support a pre-tribulation rapture, then another explanation might seem more plausible.

It seems to me there has to be somewhere in Scripture an explanation for who "he" is and what the "what" is. Consider this scenario, but be a Berean while doing so:

> There is a key to the abyss where the king of the abyss (i.e., the lawless one) is being held. The abyss is the "what" that is restraining the angel (a bad angel) of the abyss. A star is given the key to the shaft of the abyss ("key" in on the point that the key is **given** to the star). The one who gives the star the key is an angel (a good angel). The angel is the "he." The star opens the shaft of the abyss. The star who was given the key had just fallen from heaven. The star is Satan, also known as the dragon. He was thrown down from heaven to the earth just before the forty-two months of time known as the Great Tribulation. He lets the angel of the abyss out and gives to him his power, throne, and authority. The angel of the abyss is none other than the beast (the lawless one). The key ends up back in the hands of the angel who had given him the key, and he uses the key to lock Satan away in the abyss for one thousand years.

My scenario at this point is conjecture. But it seems to make sense to me, whereas the theory of the Holy Spirit doesn't seem to make sense, as I see no other Scripture that supports that their theory. If you want to be a Berean to check out my theory, read, along with 2 Thessalonians 2:1–9, Revelation 9:1–2, 11, 12:9, 13:2–7, and 20:1–3.

Section 7: Is the Day of the Lord the Great Tribulation?

This section contains what I think are two of the reasons why pre-tribulationists teach that the Day of the Lord is the Great Tribulation.

Let's first think about what 1 Thessalonians 4:15–5:2 and 2 Thessalonians 1:6–2:8 teach: The rapture will occur *on* the Day of the Lord at the end of the age. We know it will come at the end of the age because both books reveal that sinners will be destroyed on that day, and 2 Thessalonians 2:8 teaches that the man of lawlessness (the beast) will be destroyed on that day.

However, the pre-tribulation rapture theory says the rapture will take place seven years **before** the end of the age. Since it is clear that the rapture/gathering will take place on the Day of the Lord, do they work out their theory by saying that the Day of the Lord will span seven years? That way, they can teach that the rapture will take place **on** the Day of the Lord, **and** they can also teach that sinners and the beast will be destroyed seven years later **on** the Day of the Lord.

Another way to defend a pre-tribulation rapture is to teach that the Great Tribulation is the time of the Lord's wrath. Keep in mind they believe that his wrath will be poured out **during** the Great Tribulation. But is the Great Tribulation the wrath [*Strong's Concordance* 3709] of God (a specific wrath that won't be poured out until the "Great Day of Their Wrath") or is it the fury of Satan? It is not the wrath of God, as was shown in chapter 1. If it was the wrath of God, that would necessitate a pre-tribulation rapture.

Section 8: Imminent Return?

The pre-tribulationists believe in the imminent return of Jesus, and that it will occur before the days of the persecution of the saints known as the Great Tribulation. It will be a surprise to us, they say, because it will not be preceded by any signs that would alert us to his coming to rapture us.

However, this verse says it won't be a surprise to believers. It will be a surprise to unbelievers, but not to us.

> But you, brothers, are not in darkness so
> that this day should surprise you like a thief.
> (1 Thessalonians 5:4)

With regard to Jesus saying that no one knows the day or the hour, answer this question: if Jesus didn't mention the rapture in the Olivet Discourse (Matthew 24), why would he say that that no one knows the day or hour of the rapture?

And if in Matthew 24 Jesus was talking only to Jews, then why do they say he was talking to us when he said the day or the hour would not be known?

> [Jesus said,] "Then the sign of the Son of Man
> will appear in heaven and then all the tribes of
> the earth will mourn, and they will see the Son of
> Man coming on the clouds of heaven with power
> and great glory. And He will send His angels
> with a great sound of a trumpet, and they will
> gather together His elect from the four winds,
> from one end of heaven to the other. Now learn
> this parable from the fig tree: When its branch
> has already become tender and puts forth leaves,
> you know that summer is near. So you also, when
> you see all these things, know that it is near—at
> the doors! Assuredly, I say to you, this generation
> will by no means pass away till all these things
> take place. Heaven and earth will pass away, but
> My words will by no means pass away. But **of**

> **that day and hour no one knows**, not even the angels of heaven, but My Father only." (Matthew 24:29–36)

Another point I'd like to make is this: if you look at the Matthew 24 passage above, you will notice that it is the **day** we will not know. It is the **hour** we will not know. Jesus did not say that we would not know the approximate time of his coming and the rapture. In fact, he told us about signs that would precede his coming to let us know that it is near. And if you look at the Mark 13 passage below, you will notice that it's a matter of him coming "in the evening, or at midnight, or when the rooster crows, or at dawn."

> [Jesus said,] "At that time men will see the Son of Man coming in clouds with great power and glory. And he will send his angels and gather his elect from the four winds, from the ends of the earth to the ends of the heavens. Now learn this lesson from the fig tree: As soon as its twigs get tender and its leaves come out, you know that summer is near. Even so, when you see these things happening, you know that it is near, right at the door. I tell you the truth, this generation will certainly not pass away until all these things have happened. Heaven and earth will pass away, but my words will never pass away. No one knows about that day or hour, not even the angels in heaven, nor the Son, but only the Father. Be on guard! Be alert! You do not know when that time will come. It's like a man going away: He leaves his house and puts his servants in charge, each with his assigned task, and tells the one at the door to keep watch. Therefore keep watch because you do not know when the owner of the house will come back—**whether in the evening,**

or at midnight, or when the rooster crows, or at dawn." (Mark 13:26–35)

Jesus said that the days of tribulation would be cut short, or no one would survive (Mark 13:20, Matthew 24:22). Could it be that we won't know the day or the hour because he will cut short the 3.5 years of tribulation?

Section 9: The 490-Day Prophecy

Pre-tribulationists say that the Great Tribulation will last seven years and that those years are the final years of the 490-day, Daniel 9:24-27 prophecy. I too believe that the final years of this age will be the final seven years of the Daniel prophecy, although I don't believe the Great Tribulation, the time of the persecution of the saints, will last seven years. I believe it will last 3.5 years (which is the same stretch of time as a time, times, and a half a time, also forty-two months), which will begin when the abomination of desolation stands in the holy place and end when he is destroyed. See Matthew 24:15–21; Revelation 7:9–14, 13:5-10; and Daniel 7:25.

Chapter 13

The Glorious Gospel of Jesus Christ

Adam, the first man created by God, became separated from God by a single sin. Since all human beings have sinned (Romans 3:23), all are separated from God (Isaiah 59:2). However, God made a way for us start a relationship with him now and be with him forever. Jesus is the way! "But God demonstrates his own love for us in this: While we were still sinners, Christ died for us" (Romans 5:8). God holds out to us the gift of eternal life. "For the wages of sin is death [eternal separation from God], but the gift of God is eternal life in Christ Jesus our Lord" (Romans 6:23).

"He who has the Son has life; he who does not have the Son of God does not have life" (1 John 5:12). He who believes in Jesus does not fear death, for God has made it known to him that he is a child of God and has eternal life (Romans 8:16, 1 John 5:13, Ephesians 1:13–14). He knows all his sins are forgiven, washed away by the ever-so-precious blood of the Lamb, shed on a cross.

Those who don't have their sins washed away will have to pay for every wicked or impure thought, every sexual sin, all the boasting they have done, every unkind word, every lie, every selfish deed, every good deed gone undone, every "good deed" done to look good to others and/or impress God, and every other sin. They "will be punished with everlasting destruction and shut out from the presence of the Lord and from the majesty of his power on the day he comes" (2 Thessalonians 1:9–10).

Anyone who dies without Jesus will never again have an opportunity to have his sins washed away by the blood of Jesus, the Lamb of God sacrificed for us. That's why the Bible says, "now is the day of salvation" (2 Corinthians 6:2).

God gave us the Ten Commandments (i.e., the law), which can be summed up thus—love God and love your neighbor. Have you perfectly loved God? Have you bowed down to, prayed to, or worshipped anyone besides God? Have you perfectly loved and respected family members, friends, neighbors, coworkers, and strangers? Have you ever committed adultery? Have you ever caused another to sin? Have you ever paid back evil with evil instead of with good? When you were a child, did you disobey your parents?

Allow the precepts of God to humble you and convict you of sin, **for that is their purpose**. "The law was put in charge to lead us to Christ that we might be justified by faith" (Galatians 3:24). God desires to justify you, so let the knowledge of your disobedience drive you into the arms of the Savior of the world, the **only** Savior, your Creator and the Creator of all that exists, the one who died in your place.

Think about it. Jesus, who was with God and was God, came to earth from heaven and was born as a human being (John 1:1, 14). He, God in the flesh, the sinless one, died a horrible death on a cross so that you could be completely forgiven. He, now in heaven, having been raised from the dead, the Shepherd of his sheep, is longing to bring you into his fold. Humble yourself before God and ask for mercy (Luke 18:9–14). Turn to the Lord from your sins, wanting forgiveness, abandoning thoughts of trying to save yourself through religious rituals, church attendance, good deeds, prayers, or anything else. Trust in the Lord Jesus Christ to save you. If you do that, the Lord will put his Spirit in you and begin the work of lovingly and patiently molding you into the person he wants you to be. The power to do that belongs to him and him alone. We cannot love the way he wants us to until his Spirit resides in us. He is love, and all love comes from him.

The best and wisest thing you could do with your time is devour the following to find out if all of the above is true: Luke 18:9–14, Romans 1–6, Ephesians 1–2, Titus 3:3–7, the Book of Galatians, the Book of 2 Peter, the Book of Colossians, the Book of John, the Book of 2 Timothy, and the Book of Hebrews 10:11–18. If you become a follower of Jesus, you will hunger for more.

Why not call on the name of the Lord and ask for the free gift of eternal life?

> Everyone who calls on the name of the Lord will be saved. (Acts 2:21)

> "Come!" Whoever is thirsty, let him come; and whoever wishes, let him take the free gift of the water of life. (Revelation 22:17)

> Jesus answered her, "If you knew the gift of God and who it is that asks you for a drink, you would have asked him, and he would have given you living water." (John 4:10)

About the Author

Colleen began to study the Book of Revelation even before she came to know the Lord Jesus Christ. It was partly because of her fascination with end-times that she kept reading the Bible. The Lord used her desire to know more to draw her attention to Jesus. After about a year, through believing what she was reading, she came to call on the name of the Lord and was saved.

Because of her absolute devotion to the truth of God's word, she was bothered when certain teachers tried to explain away what she understood to be evidence of a post-tribulation rapture. She also saw that Paul, according to 2 Thessalonians 2:3, tells us to not let anyone deceive us in any way with regard to the timing of the rapture.

As she studied, she kept notes and eventually turned those notes into this book. The book is different than most books about the rapture in that pertinent Scriptures are presented and questions asked of them so that the reader can discover the truth for himself/herself. Chapter after chapter leads to the same conclusion: The rapture will be a post-tribulation event.

www.ingramcontent.com/pod-product-compliance
Lightning Source LLC
Chambersburg PA
CBHW031307160726
47993CB00001B/324